DECKS,
PORCHES,
AND PATIOS

Decks, Porches, and Patios

EDITED BY

GEORGE DANIELS

CHL CREATIVE HOME LIBRARY®

In Association with Better Homes and Gardens®
Meredith Corporation

CHL CREATIVE HOME LIBRARY®

© 1974 by Meredith Corporation, Des Moines, Iowa

All rights reserved
Printed in the United States of America

Library of Congress Cataloging in Publication Data

Daniels, George Emery
Decks, Porches, and Patios.

1. Decks (Architecture, Domestic) 2. Patios.
3. Porches. I. Title.
TH4970.D36 643'.55 74-7287
ISBN 0-696-13000-9

CONTENTS

HOW TO GET THE MOST OUT OF THIS BOOK

The most enjoyable outdoor living area—be it a patio, a deck, or a porch—is the one that turns out in just the way you want it. It should be ideally suited to your particular piece of property, your way of living, and your pocketbook. One of the surest—and certainly most rewarding —ways to acquire it according to your needs and specifications is to build it yourself, using your own ideas.

This book is intended to serve as a practical guide for doing just that. The methods described here are proven ones that you can adapt to your house, your land, and your budget. Unless your plans are unusually lavish, you can do the job on a pay-as-you-go basis so that when the building is done, the paying is done.

If you're a beginner—In considering this major do-it-yourself project, you'll find it encouraging to know that some of the major jobs described in the following pages have been built by beginners, even first-timers, with no major complications. Keep in mind, too, that you can hire professionals to do any one part of the job that you feel reluctant or inadequate to handle. Sometimes this is the only practical approach. If, for example, your plans call for extensive earth moving, consider hiring a professional with a bulldozer who can finish in an hour a job that might take you weeks to do.

Use the index—So that as much useful information as was possible could be put into the book's available space, subjects are not repeated. Moreover, different ways of doing the same thing are not included unless there is a good reason. Roof construction, for instance, is explained in Chapter 5, which deals with porches. But the same information applies if you want to build a roof over a patio or a deck. In any case, the index will tell you where to look. It will also lead you to a part of Chapter 6 that deals with ready-made roof structures that come in kit form, in the event that a quick and easy job is your principle aim. Remember, you are the boss on this job—so you decide how you want to do it.

There is a bonus, therefore, for those who read all the chapters, even though some of the material covers subjects you may not need to know about. There is a good chance that such chapters will tell you something of value—such as the advice offered in Chapter 6 on protection against termites. You can apply this information to your house or your garage, as well. The facts listed in Chapter 4—about ground fault interrupters for outdoor electrical outlets—can likewise eliminate a number of other possible electrical shock hazards around the house.

Naturally, when you are planning a sizable home improvement such as an outdoor living area, it pays to learn all you can about the subject before you start. This includes some things you can't find in a book. If you happen to notice a similar type of work being done in your neighborhood, try to watch what goes on. Actually observing a job in progress can tell you more than words and pictures ever can. For example, a basement floor being poured in a new house has a lot in common with making a patio slab. The framing of the house itself is much like the framing of a deck or a porch. Better still, if one of your neighbors happens to be doing the same thing that you're planning to do, talk to him about it. He may have some good tips for you. And if you've already read this book, you will definitely have some good tips for him! Exchanging ideas in this way can make it more fun—and that's what this book Decks, Porches, and Patios is all about.

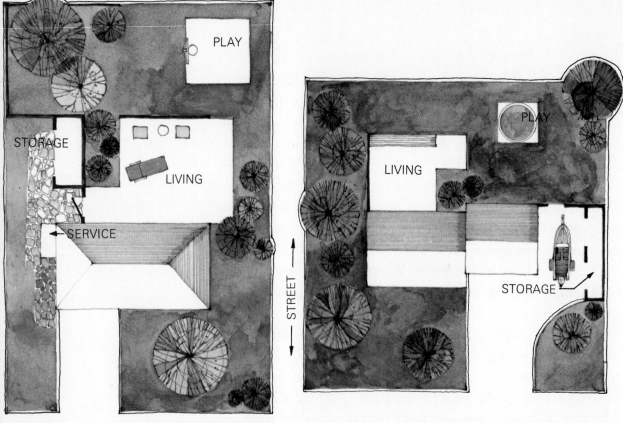

When planning an outdoor living area, the homeowner must allow sufficient setback from all property lines.

1 / ABOUT BUILDING CODES AND ZONING RESTRICTIONS

Before planning to build a deck, porch, or patio, check into any local zoning and building regulations that your community may have. They may impose certain limitations on or make certain requirements of your project. Zoning ordinances, for example, vary from one locality to another. Some simply set broad, general rules. Others state exactly what you may or may not add to your house. And the building regulations may require merely that you obtain a building permit (which is usually very easy), or they may go so far as to specify the type of materials that must be used and require an inspection of the job before it can be approved. In areas where a building permit is necessary, the application form is likely to require that you include an estimate of the cost of your deck or porch. In many areas, a representative from the tax assessor's office will look over the completed job to ascertain that your estimate was reasonably accurate. Then it will be added to the assessed value of your house and taxed on the same basis, probably on your next tax bill. The procedure varies with the locality. To get the specifics for your area, call the local tax assessor's office. More about building codes later in the book.

If the local regulations are available in printed form, as they often are for a small charge, buy a copy. You can phone the local building department or the town clerk to find out where to buy your copy.

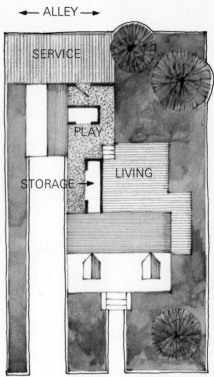

This narrow lot allows room for expansion toward the rear without violating local building regulations.

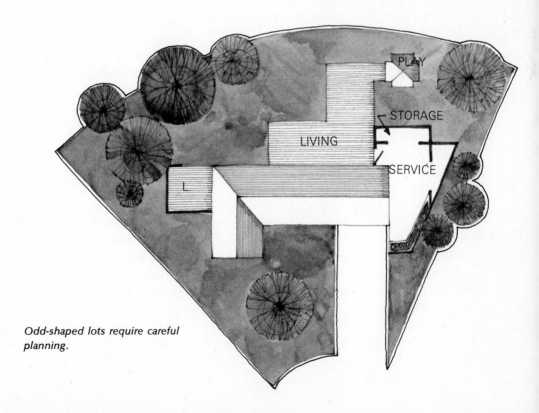

Odd-shaped lots require careful planning.

Once you know your local zoning laws and building regulations, use a 50-foot tape rule to measure the proper distance from your outdoor living area to all property lines.

About Zoning Regulations

Setbacks. Among the zoning regulations that might affect your plans are "setback" requirements. A setback is the distance that your house must be from your front, rear, and side property lines. Since a porch or deck is a part of the house, it cannot be built closer to the property lines than the setbacks allow. This ensures that adequate space will be maintained between houses.

If your house is on a narrow lot, it may already be too close to the side setbacks to allow for expansion in that direction; however, there's likely to be room for expansion at the rear. Of course, you need to know exactly where the boundary lines of your property are. Don't trust to guesswork. If the land has been surveyed and mapped, you may still be able to find the boundary markers (typically of pipe or stone) placed on it when it was surveyed. If not, try to contact the original surveyor or look for another surveyor in the same area and get from him an estimate on reestablishing the boundaries.

Although you may have been familiar with the zoning regulations of your neighborhood when you first moved in, double check. Changing conditions will often result in changes in zoning rules that you may not know about unless you have followed the local news carefully. These changes will often vary from one part of the community to another, sometimes affecting different sides of the same street. (Some of the houses shown in the photographs in this book are on streets that have been zoned differently on each side.)

Variances. If the zoning regulations present a major obstacle to your plans, you can apply for a "variance," which is an exemption to the rules. Usually, there will also be a zoning board of appeals to which you can take the matter if the variance is refused. And, finally, you can always go to court. Fortunately, there's a good chance that you'll never have to face any of these complications. Of more than a dozen new decks and porches whose construction was followed through and, in some cases, photographed while this book was being prepared, none encountered zoning problems.

About Building Codes

Once you start actually building your deck or porch, the local building code (if there is one) can be much more help than hindrance. In a way, it does the "engineering" for you, as it will usually specify the minimum lumber sizes considered safe for the basic parts of the structure. Most codes, for example, include a table giving joist (floor beam) sizes according to the planned distance between supports; in other words, heavier joists will be required for a wide deck or porch than for a narrow one. These size tables are based on typical floor loads, which can run to several tons when you add up the

Imaginative planning provides a small upper deck over the front of the carport (left) and a roomy ground-level deck behind the house (right) in this narrow-lot situation.

weight of people and deck furniture at a fair-sized cookout.

To make sure that the work follows the rules, an inspection may be required before the job can be approved. If you are doing the construction yourself and have questions about any aspect of it, such as what is the minimum allowable space between under-deck supporting posts (not always covered in codes), ask the building inspector *before* you do the work. He can answer your questions and probably offer some helpful suggestions as well. (Information on construction elsewhere in this book is based on typical requirements, but as codes may vary, follow your local regulations.)

One other factor to consider is the location of the septic tank and absorption field. If your house has this type of system, *no* structure—porches and decks included—

should be built over it. If the house is fairly new, you may be able to get the specific location of tank and field from the builder. If you can't find a source of this information, look in your basement for the exit point of the building drain—the final section of large drainage plumbing that leads outside to the septic tank and field. A little exploratory digging outward from the house—in line with the drain and to about the same depth—will usually locate the tank. (You should know the tank location anyway, in case it should ever need to be pumped out.) From there on, a septic tank servicing company is likely to be your best bet in locating the approximate boundaries of your absorption field.

Patios. Whether a patio or paved terrace is subject to the same regulations as decks and porches depends on the particular set of regulations. In some instances, the patio is regarded as a part of the house only if it is made in such a way that it could serve as the foundation of an added room. A poured concrete slab patio, for example, would be in that category, though one made of patio block or brick, laid in sand, would not be. Inquire about the regulations that apply to patios before you decide on the materials you'll use. If you don't plan to enclose it later on and you can avoid legal complications merely by selecting certain materials, you may want to do it that way.

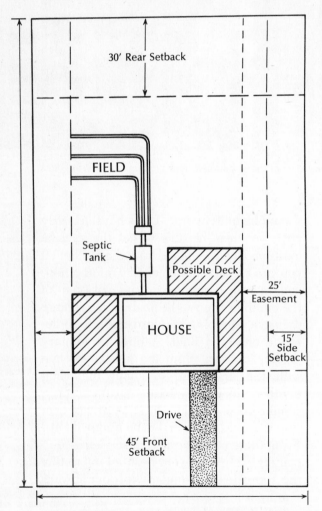

This sketch shows how your outdoor living possibilities can be affected by an easement. Be sure to check your deed first.

About Deeds

If you left the details of your deed to your lawyer when you bought your house, it would be wise to read the deed now before you build any additions. Ask your lawyer about anything you don't understand in the deed. The chances are that the deed won't restrict or block your plans, though some deeds might. For example, some deeds are so specific as to prohibit a homeowner from having a clothesline on his property.

Easements. A feature of some deeds that may affect your porch or deck plans is called an easement. This permits someone other than you to use your property or a part of it

Even in a well-planned residential development such as the one pictured here, you must give careful attention to local building restrictions before adding on a deck, porch, or patio.

for some specific purpose. For example, some previous owner of the property may have given an easement to the water company, permitting it to lay a water main under a part of the lawn and allow it access to the property in order to maintain or repair the water main. Obviously, you don't want to discover suddenly that you have built your deck over a portion of the lawn through which a bulldozer is about to pass in the course of repairing the water main. So it's wise to know your deed thoroughly. In some rare cases, an easement granted long ago may not be evident in your current deed. In such instances a title search conducted when you buy the property should bring it to light.

All information about your property and the local regulations that affect it can be important to you for many reasons. If you acquire it as a result of planning a sun deck, then your deck has already served a worthwhile purpose.

2 / CHOOSING THE RIGHT LOCATION FOR YOUR OUTDOOR LIVING AREA

Purely from the standpoint of comfort and convenience, how do you select the best location for a deck, a porch, or a patio? To start, let's assume that the location of your house is in that happy category whereby you can attach the outdoor addition to the front, the back, or either side with no particular problem.

The best location for either an open deck or patio depends on how you plan to use it. Is it to be an area for family dining and entertaining out of doors? Or is it intended to be a haven for sunbathers? Perhaps you'd like to have it serve both purposes. In any event, here are a few points to consider:

If quick shade is required for a sun-baked patio location, an overhead lattice is one excellent way to get it. Supports are cut from old telephone poles, which are often available from your local phone company.

Land Contour

If the land around your home is reasonably level, your planning will be simple; but if it slopes, you may have a problem. For example, if the area on which you'd like to have a patio happens to slope steeply toward the house, you may want to consider having it leveled. Check your Yellow Pages under "Contractors-Excavating," and arrange for a contractor to look at the area; he can then decide what type of machine can do the job best. (A small machine will, of course, cost less than a big one.) A machine with a "blade" on the front simply pushes the earth ahead of it in order to level off the area. This will do the job well so long as there is a place to which the earth can be pushed and leveled off.

If the area is pocketed by house, garage, or shrubbery, a machine with a "loader" instead of a blade is usually the answer. This type can scoop up the earth, hold it in its loader scoop, and carry it away—backward, if necessary. Usually, you pay for such work by the hour, counting from the time the machine and its operator leave the contractor's headquarters until they return.

Level ground made this large deck possible to build using simple construction techniques (see Chapter 4). An umbrella shades the table in early afternoon, while shade trees take over later in the day. The deck area is large enough for both dining and dancing.

This combination multilevel deck and patio makes the most of sloping terrain and creates an unusual effect. You can achieve this by adapting some of the methods described in Chapters 3 and 4.

A good idea is to watch for one of these machines working on property near yours and then ask the operator if he can take on your job next. If he can, you can probably save the cost of at least a one-way trip between the contractor's and your property by making a deal with him.

Although earth-moving work isn't cheap, most homeowners who haven't looked into it before find that it doesn't cost as much as they expected. To get the best bargain, ask your neighbors about good excavating contractors. Also phone a few contractors and

ask for their rates, including the probable cost of getting the machine to your location.

Before hiring anyone to do work on your property, however, ask your insurance agent about coverage in case of accident. Your best bet is a fully insured contractor. Find out about this before you settle on the final arrangements.

Sun versus Shade

If your open deck or patio is to be used in the daytime as an outdoor dining and entertaining area, you should favor a shady spot.

A few basic techniques help keep this patio's shade tree healthy. The brick floor, which has been laid in sand around the base of the tree wall, slopes gently toward it. The wall itself has uncemented openings.

Hot sun makes a poor appetizer. Shade can be provided ideally by a shade tree located close to the house, if you're fortunate enough to have one. Lacking such a tree, your shade can come from the shadow of the house itself, on the north side. Just how far this shadow will extend outward from the house depends, of course, on the height of the house. In any event, locating your deck or patio there will help eliminate the glare and wall-reflected heat of the sun.

For your information: When planning your deck or patio, be sure to measure the width of this shaded area—but do it during the spring–summer season. In winter, the shadow of your house is much larger than in summer because the winter sun is lower in the sky. Measuring then could cause you to make a costly mistake in terms of future comfort. At the same time, keep track of the shade area on the east side of your house during the afternoon, which is the time

when most of your outdoor daytime entertaining is likely to take place. As the sun moves lower in the latter part of the day, the shaded area on the east side of your house will expand. This means that a deck or patio extending around the northeast corner of your house is most likely to have something for everybody. In the morning hours, for example, the eastern section, unshaded by trees, can become a haven for family sunbathers (morning sun is tanning sun). A northwest corner location will provide the same shade on its north section and afternoon sun on the west section—this is often welcome in spring and fall when shady areas tend to be chilly.

Your house, of course, may not face due north or south. But whatever its orientation, you can still use its shadow. Do consider this factor when you plan an open deck or patio. It may save you the cost of an awning or other type of sun shield.

Most houses face the street; in housing developments they are often located fairly close to it. This means that you may not be able to build your deck or patio according to the dictates of the sun. If your house is on the south side of the street, for example, a deck or patio built on its north side (space permitting) would, in most cases, be too close to the street for any semblance of privacy. And the situation probably wouldn't be much better on the sides. So your outdoor living is likely to be limited to the back of the house—the south side—where you'll undoubtedly want to provide shade by one means or another.

For patios located close to the property line, a privacy fence may be the answer. Homeowners with adjoining land often share the cost of these fences.

Porches

A roofed porch, of course, provides its own shade. But it will also block direct sunlight from the house windows under the roof. You may find this pleasant in the summer, for its cooling effect, but you will miss the sunlight in the winter.

To compromise, plan your porch so that at least a portion of its floor area will be shaded in summer and sunny in winter. You can do this simply by taking advantage of the difference in seasonal positions. Because the relative height of the sun varies with the latitude of your location, as well as with the season, the most accurate way—assuming that you can plan far enough ahead—is to measure the shadow positions beforehand in both summer and winter.

An often-overlooked bonus sometimes possible with a roofed-porch plan is that an upstairs sun deck is possible. If bedroom or hallway windows look out on a porch roof, for example, a pair of them can usually be replaced with French doors. In that case, build the porch roof with suitable surface, and you will have an all-day sun deck for little more than the price of the roof alone. Include a railing, of course, and keep the design in harmony with the house. An upstairs deck can also add a fire-safety factor; it's easier to slide down one of the supporting posts than to drop from a second-floor window.

Alternatives to the roofed porch include removable awnings, usually higher priced than a permanent roof, and fast-growing shade trees. Check the local price of trees suitable to your area. You may find it possible to buy two or three with fairly large trunk diameters (3½ inches or so) for about the same price as an awning and frame. If you

*A large-windowed porch that opens onto a **deck** can solve the problem of sudden showers by making it easy to move an outdoor party indoors quickly. It also provides a comfortable year-round shelter.*

For privacy and shade, a simple square-patterned trellis of 1 × 2's can be built around a patio or low deck. A trellis like the one shown here is easy and inexpensive to build.

live in a winter snow area, however, avoid those tree species that are known to be too weak to sustain serious ice-storm damage.

The House Floor Plan

Although it may not always be possible, having direct access from a dining deck or patio to the kitchen is a worthwhile feature. Entertaining tends to lose its appeal when one has to carry dinner for eight on a lengthy trip through the house or down a flight of stairs—and then later have to repeat the same course with a load of dirty dishes.

Some "raised ranch" and split-level homes have rear kitchens and back doors that are actually on the second-floor level, with stairs leading to the ground. In that case, it's wise to rule out a ground-level patio in favor of a deck at the kitchen level. Homeowners who do their own deck-building often use the original stairs, relocated, from the new deck to the ground.

When the only feasible deck or patio location is on a side of the house other than the side on which the door to the kitchen or indoor dining area is located, consider add-

The raised-level deck at left has been built over a hard-to-remove rock formation.

nates sun problems. For daytime comfort, you can provide quick localized shade simply and easily by setting up an umbrella table. You can even arrange for an artificial breeze with the aid of an electric fan, like the old overhead model shown (sometimes available from building wreckers), a floor or window fan, or an attic type protected by a mesh guard. Often overlooked by home-owners, outdoor fan-cooling was frequently used on restaurant dining terraces before the days of widespread air conditioning.

It may be, too, that the best location for a patio is somewhere *away* from the house, perhaps because of an attractive view or a prevalent breeze. If it is to be within reasonable walking distance of the house, such an arrangement can be entirely practical. It may, for example, have the benefit of shade trees not found close to the house. All too often, mass-unit builders cut trees from an oversized area when clearing land for a house, and as a result all worthwhile shade trees are located some distance away. If possible, connect the patio to the house with a patio block walk. This provides a path smooth enough for a patio cart, and thus makes transportation of the essentials for outdoor entertaining a relatively easy task.

One away-from-the-house location that often works out well is the area behind a garage, attached or otherwise. In that case, another overhead-type door—similar to the conventional car entrance door—can be installed in the rear wall of the garage. With such an opening leading out to the patio, you have an indoor–outdoor combination that enables you to transfer your cookout into the garage—and still have plenty of room for tables, chairs, and guests—in case of a sudden rainstorm.

ing a walk-width section around a corner of the house to the door. In some cases, it may be simpler to add a new door at a point that provides as nearly direct access to the kitchen as possible. This can be a do-it-yourself job in most cases.

Many decks and patios, of course, are used largely in the evening, which elimi-

A simple trellis roof made of painted 4 × 4 posts and 2 × 4 rafters, with 2 × 2's nailed across top, highlights this small but elegant patio.

Fortunately, it's not too difficult to imagine what your proposed deck or patio will look and feel like—simply relax for a few minutes in a comfortable deck chair at the proposed location. If the traffic noise level seems high, shrubbery or evergreens between you and the street can do a lot to muffle it. A woven wood or louvered fence can serve the same purpose without blocking the breeze. Either way, you'll have more privacy. And there's always the chance, of course, that the location will turn out to have no problems at all. At that point, you can stop relaxing—and get to work!

This deck structure made with patio-type materials creates the effect of an extended patio. The open-grid roof, with spaced plastic panels, offers shade; the bench-railing combination in the rear completes the design.

3 / HOW TO BUILD YOUR OWN PATIO

A patio has certain advantages over a deck or a porch. For one, it can blend more easily with the landscape. And from the practical point of view, it's likely to be easier and less expensive to build. The overall price and the building time depend on the materials used and the size of the patio. In the easiest and lowest-priced category, attractive average-sized patios costing about as much as a high-grade automobile tire have been ready for use within minutes after the materials arrived. Other, more complicated types can involve several days work and cost four or five times as much. The most popular methods and materials will lie somewhere between these two extremes.

Shade trees and patio block laid in sand set the theme for this colorful table setting. Luxurious as it is, the plan is not difficult to copy; all you need is a shady place near the house.

A combination of gravel and concrete paves this patio nicely. Bent strips of 1 × 2 with short spacers (also 1 × 2) make up the curved bench top. A framing of 2 × 4 stock supports the structure.

Gravel Patios

What we often refer to as gravel is more commonly known to building suppliers as crushed stone, and it is specified according to the average size of the pieces. (During production, stones are separated according to size by being passed through a mesh that has openings of various sizes.) Half-inch size is widely used for patios (and driveways) because it's comfortable to walk on (heels don't sink in as they do on finer sizes) and it is less likely to cause accidents than are the larger sizes.

How to buy gravel. Like sand, you buy crushed stone by the cubic yard and you get the best price when you buy a full truckload, which may be as little as 4 yards (ample for most patios), depending on the size of the truck. If you need less than a load, ask about the per-yard price difference—it's usually quite moderate.

How to estimate the amount. Once you have decided on the size of your patio, it's easy to estimate the amount of crushed stone you will need to cover it. Figure on a depth of about 2 inches, some of which will become embedded in the earth. Then, think of a cubic yard as an actual yard-square cube, and you'll see that you can get eighteen 2-inch-thick slices from it, or 19 square yards. So you buy as many cubic yards as you need to provide enough 2-inch-thick slices. It's as simple as that.

The easiest way. In advance, remove the sod from the patio area with a spade (or sod lifter, if you have one) and use it elsewhere —such as on bald areas in your lawn. Cover the area from which the sod has been removed with 45-pound roofing felt (like heavy tar paper). This will minimize the chance of new grass or weeds working their way up through the crushed stone. (The roofing felt will probably acquire some rips and holes later, but it will retard the sprouts.) If the weather is windy, hold the felt down with some small stones until the gravel arrives.

How to Spread It

If the patio area is located in a place where the gravel truck can drive over it and if the driver is experienced, you can avoid most of the gravel-spreading work. The truck can move slowly across the patio area, spreading a layer of gravel as it goes. All you have to do is rake out any unevenness. For this, use an iron rake turned upside down (tines up). Total laying and raking time on a typical truck-laid gravel patio: 20 minutes.

If the truck is unable to drive over to the patio area for one reason or another, have the gravel dumped in a pile as close to the patio area as possible. (Be *sure* the truck doesn't pass over any part of your septic tank or the drainage field that goes with it.)

If the gravel load is relatively small, you can move it to the patio area a batch at a time in a wheelbarrow. If you have a garden tractor and a trailer cart for it, you can haul the gravel in that: It will hold the muscle work to a reasonable level even on fairly large loads. But you will still have to shovel the entire load of gravel into the wheelbarrow or cart. Since each cubic yard weighs approximately a ton and a quarter, you will have your work

cut out for you. One good leisurely solution is to hire somebody with a small power loader to do the job. (See hiring details in Chapter 2.) Machines of this type—especially tractors with wheels instead of crawler treads—can usually maneuver with success around sensitive areas like septic tank fields when carrying heavy materials like gravel. (Don't have this kind of work done when the ground is soft, as after rainy spring weather.)

Once the gravel has been transported to the patio area by whatever method, spread it evenly with a shovel and rake it level.

About drainage. Whatever you use to surface a patio, be sure to grade the surface gently in a direction that will carry rainwater *away* from the house or toward one end—for example, where the patio runoff passes down a driveway gutter. The slope should be just enough to prevent water from puddling (about ¼ inch per foot); this can be easily arranged with a "line" level, which is a small, inexpensive bubble-type level that clips to a string held taut between two stakes, as shown in the diagram.

Line level, above. In grading, remove soil until surface is parallel to slope line (see below).

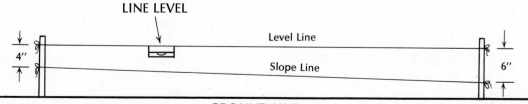

LINE LEVEL

4"

Level Line

Slope Line

6"

GROUND LINE

A geometric pattern of crushed stone and concrete surfaces this patio's open area. The roof built over the covered portion is supported by 6 × 6 posts bolted to top framework.

The drawbacks. Although usually at the low end of the price scale, the gravel patio isn't as easy on the feet as a hard-surfaced one and metal furniture with small-diameter legs will tend to tip on it. Many gravel patios, however, have been in regular, successful use for years; if you're uncertain whether you'd like one, look for a gravel driveway the next time you're out riding through a residential area. Try walking on it—give it a good eye and foot test to make sure it's what you want.

To minimize some of the problems caused by gravel, various types of patio block can be used in combination with it. For example, large round patio blocks—sometimes called bubble stones—can be placed at furniture locations so that chair and table legs will rest on them. Also, rectangular blocks can be used to pave the "traffic" and dining areas of the patio, with gravel covering the remaining, major portion of the area for economy. Bricks, of course, can serve the same purpose as blocks.

Half-blocks (right) make a straight edge when used with Spanish tile pattern patio blocks.

Patio-Block Patios

The increasing popularity of patio block has resulted in new block forms being made available in many geographical areas. The old familiar size and shape is the 8 × 16-inch block, in either a 1½- or 2-inch thickness. But you can also find 16-inch square blocks, hexagonals, and Spanish tile forms. Half-blocks and fill-ins are also available to enable a patio constructed with elaborate tile shapes to have straight edges. The usual colors include natural (usually priced lower than colors), yellow, green, red, and sometimes "dark" (which approaches black). Still other colors are available at some outlets.

How to buy blocks. You can compute how many blocks you will need by using simple arithmetic and a measuring tape. The price is not likely to shock you, either. You'll probably save a sizable amount if you bring the blocks home instead of having them delivered, but you'll have to make several trips (especially with a small car) because the 2-inch-thick 8 × 16-inch blocks weigh about 17 pounds each and the 16-inch square ones are 34 pounds. So ten rectangular blocks will weigh as much as a husky passenger—which is a good way to compute your car's hauling capacity. Be sure to ask the weight of the blocks you buy, as it sometimes varies.

How to lay blocks. The easiest way to lay patio blocks is on a base of sand. It's much easier to level and smooth a sand surface than an average soil surface. Of course, if the soil is easily worked, like some sandy soils, you don't need the extra sand layer.

If you do need a layer of sand, here is the procedure: First, remove a little more than 3 inches of sod. This will allow for about a 1½-inch layer of sand and 2-inch-thick blocks. The top surface of the blocks should not be more than half an inch above the normal soil surface of the lawn—otherwise, you'll find yourself tripping over the edge of the patio.

If you do *not* use sand, remove only enough sod to equal the thickness of the block. Avoid a depth that places the upper surface of the blocks below the surrounding soil surface, for this can cause puddling.

Whether or not you need a layer of sand, you can use the roofing felt, as with the gravel, directly over the soil to prevent

A dry wall retains sandy fill to make a level patio over sloping ground.

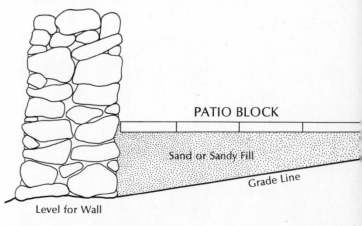

PATIO BLOCK

Sand or Sandy Fill

Grade Line

Level for Wall

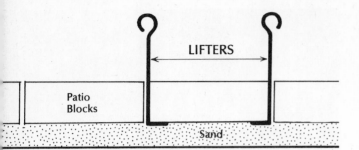

LIFTERS

Patio
Blocks

Sand

Wire lifters are used to remove individual patio blocks laid in sand. If patio benches and tables (below) are wobbly, this step is necessary to correct unevenness.

weeds from growing between the tiles. Since this isn't as much of a problem with patio block as it is with gravel, you may decide to omit the felt and lick the weeds simply by squirting plant killer between the blocks wherever a weed or blade of grass appears.

Assuming that you have a sand base, use an inverted iron rake to smooth and grade it to a slight pitch (⅛ to ¼ inch per foot) away from the house so that rainwater can flow freely across the smooth surface for runoff. Use a line level for the job.

Starting from a corner of the prepared area, lay the blocks a row at a time. If an individual block wobbles on the sand or lies above or below its neighbor, use a garden trowel to add or remove as much sand as is necessary to make it firm and even with adjacent blocks. (If you lay blocks directly on the soil, use loose soil for leveling.) Set the blocks against each other (not too tightly) and don't worry about gaps of a quarter-inch or so. These are likely to occur occasionally because of slight variations on the blocks.

If, after the patio is completed, a block must be lifted from the inside area in order to correct wobbliness or unevenness, you can simplify the job by making three simple wire lifters. These are 8-inch lengths of galvanized iron wire (about as thick as pencil lead) with a half-inch L bend at one end and a finger-sized loop at the other. Push two of them down, L end first, on opposite sides of the block, and turn them until the L's are hooked under the block. Then repeat the process with the third wire on one of the other sides. (The lifters fit down easily between the blocks.) You can then lift two of the wires while a helper lifts the third, and the block will emerge easily without disturbing its neighbors. Use a trowel to level and adjust the sand base as necessary, and then replace the block, using the lifters to lower it back into place. Keep the lifters handy in case another block settles unevenly; this is a common occurrence with newly built patios.

Patio block can be used to suit any style. The same patio blocks, laid in sand in the same basic pattern, pave the patio at left as well as the one on the right.

These bricks were laid in dry cement mortar mix over a slab and then water-soaked with hose spray to ensure fast, effective setting.

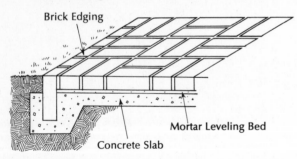

Brick Edging

Mortar Leveling Bed

Concrete Slab

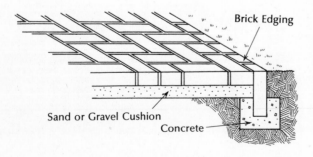

Brick Edging

Sand or Gravel Cushion

Concrete

Brick Patios

If your brick is standard size, you can figure four-and-a-half bricks for each square foot of patio area. Bricks make a very attractive patio, but if you live in a winter freeze area, be sure that the type you use can take it. (Grade SW has a high degree of frost resistance.)

Follow the same procedure for laying brick on sand as described for laying patio block. Because there will be more space between bricks than between the patio blocks, however, there will obviously be

Brick edging set in fresh concrete rims a channel built around patio and prevents bricks laid in sand from slipping apart.

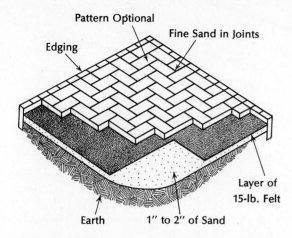

Pattern Optional

Fine Sand in Joints

Edging

Layer of
15-lb. Felt

Earth   1″ to 2″ of Sand

Brick edging (above) embedded directly in soil. Asphalt felt prevents weeds from growing up between bricks.

more opportunities for weeds to grow—so you'll probably need that layer of roofing felt mentioned earlier.

Flagstone Patios

Flagstone is a widely used term that refers to a broad range of natural paving stones. You can locate a local supplier under "Mason Contractor's Equipment and Supplies" in your Yellow Pages. The type of stone avail-

A few possible brick paving patterns. Bricks can be cut with a chipping hammer or masonry blade.

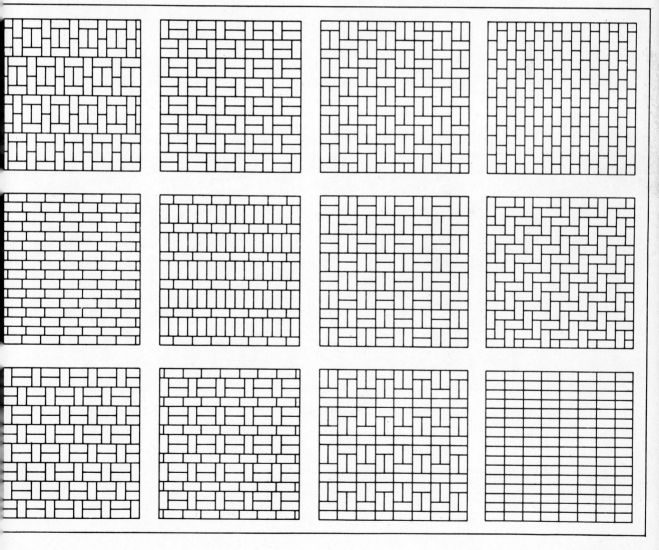

The shadow pattern formed by the open rafters covering this brick patio creates a cooling effect despite the absence of shade trees overhead.

Shade and sun from open areas and overhanging tree boughs intermingle to give this brick and   bubble stone   patio charming versatility.

able will depend on your geographic location. Slate is one that's widely available in several colors; it's usually sold by the pound either in random shapes that fit together like a jigsaw puzzle or in rectangular-cut pieces. Its typical thickness is ¾ inch. Bluestone is another paving type that is sold in assorted rectangular sizes. Whatever type you select, it's likely to cost considerably more than patio blocks. It does make a very attractive surface, however, and it can be laid in the same way as the blocks—although the random shapes will require some extra time for fitting.

Patterns. The random-cut rectangular sizes of paving stone are usually dimensioned to "come out even" over a space of a few feet. Of course, they must be matched properly. With brick or rectangular patio block, you can select from a variety of laying patterns, as shown in the diagrams. Patio block shapes—such as hexagonal and Spanish tile—fit together naturally in their own ways, but don't forget to buy enough half-blocks or filler blocks to make straight patio edges and square corners.

Paving patterns (above and below) that leave "pinked" or notched edges (in contrast to the straight border) can be filled in with sand.

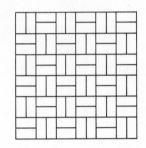 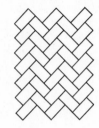

Finishing a Block, Brick, or Stone Patio

Whatever surfacing material you use (except gravel), spread some clean sand over the finished job and brush it around with a push broom so that it sifts into any gaps between blocks, bricks, or paving stones. Then sweep up the excess.

During a cold winter, patio blocks, bricks, and paving stones may "heave" in a few places as a result of ground freezing. Once the weather has warmed up, these heaved areas will almost always settle back to their original level condition without any assistance. In fact, assistance may only cause trouble, so let nature take its course.

Concrete Patios

A poured concrete slab patio can later become the floor of an added room if you plan

This poolside patio was built with random-cut paving stones set in concrete.

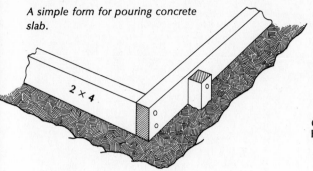

A simple form for pouring concrete slab.

2 × 4

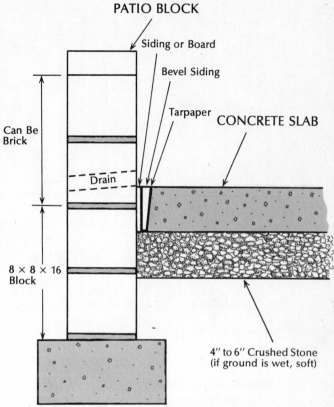

PATIO BLOCK

Siding or Board

Bevel Siding

Tarpaper

CONCRETE SLAB

Can Be Brick

Drain

8 × 8 × 16 Block

4″ to 6″ Crushed Stone (if ground is wet, soft)

Drawing shows a slab patio rimmed by a cemented wall. Wall drains are installed on the low side. Slab is kept separate from wall until dry. Remove boards later and fill gap with tar.

with that possibility in mind. Except in extremely cold climates, the thickness of the concrete should be about 4 inches. To make a form for this thickness, use stock 2 × 4 lumber set on edge and nailed to stakes placed about 4 feet apart. If the patio is eventually to be used as the floor of an average-sized room, it's best to pour it as a single slab. If it is to be a permanent patio, however, you can pave the area one part at a time, in squares or rectangles separated by a wooden gridwork. The gridwork, which also serves as the forms for pouring, can remain in place if it is made of redwood or chemically treated rot-proofed wood. Using wood gridwork will simplify the pouring of very large areas because it will enable you to work from the dry ground of adjacent squares when spreading and "screeding" the fresh concrete (see diagrams).

How to buy concrete. Concrete is sold by the cubic yard if you buy it delivered by a mixer truck—it's the easiest way if you are laying a large slab in a single pouring. Figure out the amount you will need in the same way as was described for gravel, and allow 5 to 10 percent extra for spillage over the forms. Tell your supplier you want a concrete mix for a patio. If you're in a cold winter area, ask for "air entrained" concrete. This type contains a chemical that forms millions of tiny bubbles in the concrete, which gives it much greater resistance to freeze damage. In case you end up with

some surplus, plan a use for it, such as pouring a step, a short walkway, etc. The reason for this advance planning is simple: If you don't use the excess concrete before it hardens, you will have a very major problem on your hands!

SCREEDING WITH BOARD

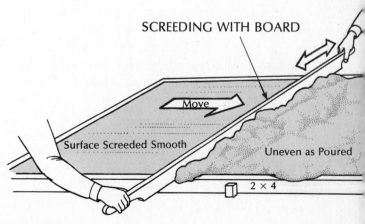

Move

Surface Screeded Smooth

Uneven as Poured

2 × 4

This tree-shaded patio began as a single row of small slabs in a redwood grid, then was expanded to the full area shown. This method allows you to do the job as time permits.

If you plan to lay your concrete in small sections in a wooden gridwork, you can rent a small cement mixer. Check your local tool rental agencies for rates. (You'll find them in the Yellow Pages under "Tools-Rental.")

If you mix your own concrete, follow the proportions listed here for each bag of cement: 1 part portland cement, 2¼ parts sand, 3 parts gravel (preferably around ½-inch size), and 5 gallons of water. (These are recommended proportions for patio use.) A standard bag of cement weighs 94 pounds and equals one cubic foot. (In Canada, the bag may be an 80-pounder.)

An easy way to measure the ingredients is with a cubical box made from ¾-inch plywood and measuring a foot square and a foot high on the inside. The proportions are based on wet sand, because sand is usually stored out of doors and therefore absorbs considerable rain, which increases its bulk. If the sand is merely damp, decrease the amount of sand slightly and increase the water slightly. If the sand is extremely wet, use a little more sand and a little less water.

(Your sand supplier will know the condition of the sand; be sure to ask his advice.) A good bet is to mix a small trial batch so that you'll be sure your concrete is easy to work with. If it's too stiff or too soft, you can adjust proportions for the main job.

Preparing the job. Remove the sod and enough soil so that your patio surface is flush with the surrounding soil or very slightly above it. Dig out any "mushy" areas, and fill them in with sand or gravel. (In heavy clay or poorly drained, wet soil, lay a 4- to 6-inch subbase of sand or crushed stone and pour the concrete on top of it.) Build the form around the patio perimeter, and use the line level to give it a slight pitch away from the house (see page 27). You are now ready to order (or prepare) the concrete.

If the concrete is delivered by mixer truck, you can probably have it brought in the day after you order it. But be sure you know exactly when it's coming. Have all your tools ready (plus a helper, if you can find one). If the concrete is to be laid on top of a sand layer, wet the sand before pouring

This sunny patio of slabs in wood gridwork was completed with one mixer-truckload. The fresh concrete was kept completely covered with polyethylene sheeting to hold moisture in until the surface cured.

When the rectangles of a patio's wooden gridwork are relatively small, 2 × 3's are sometimes used to cut costs and make each individual slab thinner. Like patio blocks, small thin slabs are less subject to cracking.

the concrete. This will prevent the sand from absorbing water from the concrete and thus weakening it. In *all* concrete slab work—large or small—you must keep the concrete moist for at least five days after it has become firm enough to sprinkle with water. This moist-curing is essential for full concrete strength. Protect it from hot sun with a covering of straw or burlap; this will also help hold the sprinkling of water that keeps it moist. An overcovering of polyethylene sheeting will also prevent evaporation.

Brick on Concrete Patios

If you want the rigidity of a concrete slab patio—particularly if you plan to enclose it later—but you prefer a brick or flagstone surface, the answer is simple: Pour the concrete slab in the usual way, but limit it to a 3-inch thickness in order to minimize costs. The layer of brick or flagging on top of the slab will add enough strength to make up for the decrease in slab thickness. You can use 2 × 3 stock for the forms, with a half-inch of soil packed tightly under them. Allow the concrete to set firm; then lay the bricks or flagging on top in mortar. Trowel the mortar so that the upper surfaces of the bricks or flagstones are smooth and even. Follow the moist-curing method described earlier for the plain concrete slab.

If the slab, plain or paved, is to be enclosed later, the foundation for the walls enclosing it can be built around it (see page 37). *First check your local building code before you pour the patio.* Some codes require a specific type of foundation that must be built before the slab is poured.

Wood Patios

Rot-resistant woods—such as redwood or wood that has been chemically rot-proofed—may be used on top of a well-drained bed of crushed stone to create the effect of a wood-surfaced patio. Good drainage, however, is essential. And to ensure rapid drying after rain, you should use decking strips that are relatively narrow (up to 2 × 4) with ¼ inch of space between them for easy circulation of air.

Remove the sod and soil to a depth of about 4 inches for the crushed stone. Again, pitch the bottom of the desodded area away from the house, preferably to drain tiles that will carry away drain-off completely. The wood decking should be *above* the level of the surrounding soil.

About Trees

If your patio is to be built around an existing shade tree and is to be surfaced with any material that carries off rainwater, especially concrete, be sure to allow ample open space around the tree. This is necessary to allow adequate water to reach the tree roots. The patio area immediately adjacent to the open space around the tree may also be pitched slightly toward it.

4 / ALL ABOUT DECKS

The simplest way to build an average-sized deck is in the same general way that the floors of your house are built. If there's a local building code in your area, it's likely that you'll be required to build your deck in that way. For a firsthand look at the details, examine the ceiling of your basement (if you have an unfinished basement) or the floor of any new house under construction near you. The drawings in this chapter show the details of a typical form of deck construction, along with other types commonly used for outdoor living areas.

This versatile deck is sunny on one side, shady on the other, with a small walkway to connect them. Space under both decks serves as a ground level living area located in cool shade. These ideas are well worth considering in planning your deck.

Lumber

All lumber is stock sized and is available at any lumberyard. The decking boards, which are usually 2 × 6 with a 3/16-inch space between them, are laid across the joists parallel to the house wall.

If there is no local code in your area, use the lumber sizes shown in the chart as a guide. Although these boards may not be as heavy as those found in the house itself, they are frequently used for deck construction. If the deck is to be enclosed at a later date—to become a playroom for the children, for example—its construction should match that of the house. Use the chart of typical building code joist sizes, or measure the size

Lumber size floor joists	Spacing center to center	Maximum span between supports
2 x 6	12 inches	10 feet
	16 inches	9 feet
	24 inches	8 feet
2 x 8	12 inches	13 feet
	16 inches	12 feet
	24 inches	10½ feet
Lumber size roof rafters		
2 x 4	12 inches	8 feet
	16 inches	7 feet
	24 inches	5¾ feet
2 x 6	12 inches	12½ feet
	16 inches	10¾ feet
	24 inches	9 feet
2 x 8	12 inches	16 feet
	16 inches	14 feet
	24 inches	12 feet

Lumber sizes recommended for floor load of 30 lbs. per square foot. If there's a local code in your area, use the sizes it specifies. Lighter lumber is sometimes permitted for some porch and deck construction. Check with your local building inspector.

of those used in your own home, assuming that they are exposed in the basement. If there is a local code, of course, you must follow it.

Storage Space

When the space under the deck is to be used for storage—ideal for lawn and garden equipment—make the decking of ⅝-inch exterior plywood instead of the spaced 2 × 6's. And pitch the deck about ¼ inch per foot (or 1 inch for every 4 feet) away from the house. Plan the deck so that all plywood panel seams that run parallel to the joists (beams) meet along a joist. Use resorcinol glue to seal and reinforce the seams. (This glue, widely used in boat building, is available at hardware stores and boatyards.) Seams that run crosswise of the joists should be covered underneath with 1 × 3 or 1 × 4

Corner bench is of stock-size framing lumber, stained.

This deck (under construction) will be open at left, enclosed at right, with joists and posts arranged accordingly.

lumber cut to fit between the joists, and then nailed. These should also be reinforced and sealed with the same glue to add overall strength.

To make doubly sure of having a dry storage area, cover the upper surface of each seam with fiber glass tape 4 inches wide, bonded to the plywood (before painting) with the same polyester resin used in boatwork, or with a "water-phase" epoxy, if available in your area. The water-phase epoxy can even be used over paint, if the paint is sound. Seams protected in this way will still be watertight after years of exposure to summer sun and winter ice.

The First Step

After you've checked the local regulations and decided on the location of your deck (see Chapters 1 and 2), the first step in the actual job consists of simple measurement. Mark the points where the ends of the deck will meet the house, and measure outward from these points, at right angles to the house

Post footings are set in line with bolts embedded, head down, and braced until concrete hardens.

wall, to the point where the outer corners of the deck will be. If you plan to use plywood in any part of the construction, you can use a plywood panel as a square.

Post Spacing

Drive stakes at the corner points to indicate where holes must be dug for the deck corner-post footings. Then, on a straight line between the corner posts, mark off locations for intermediate posts. If you plan to enclose

This hardened footing is shown with bolt ready for the post.

A hole drilled into post base fits over the bolt.

the space under the deck, place the intermediate posts so that the sheathing panels which form the walls—typically 4 × 8 plywood—will meet at the posts. If your local code permits, space them 4 feet apart and place a 2 × 4 stud between each pair.

If the space under the deck will not be enclosed, however, posts can be spaced 6 to 7 feet apart. It may be necessary to vary this so that spacing comes out even and so that the posts pass to one side or the other of the joists in your house-floor construction.

Check your local building code for footing requirements. Unless large footings are required you may be able to make the footing and masonry base for each post as a single poured unit. Just dig a hole about 18″ square to slightly below frost depth. Build a wood form around it to about 8″ above the ground, and fill the hole and the form with concrete. Embed a bolt, head down, as shown in the photos, or use an embedded bracket. The requirements for the bottom area of the footings may be figured on a certain number of pounds of load for each square foot of deck area, or on another basis, according to the code. Where large footings are required,

they are usually poured first. Then a somewhat smaller masonry column is built up from them to about 8″ above ground level, or all the way to a low deck. Code permitting, you can use 4 × 4 or 4 × 6 post for decks of average size and height. When in doubt, use the heavier size.

Construction

The simplest way to learn the fundamentals of building a deck is to follow the sequence of diagrams on page 47. You may vary the procedure if necessary to suit your individual situation.

If the deck you plan to build is neither too large nor too high and if you have a helper or two, the floor frame can be built on the ground first and then lifted to its above-ground position (see Diagram A, page 48). This simplifies the assembly because the nails that hold the joists between the headers (see Diagram B, page 48) can then be driven through the headers into the ends of the joists. This makes for a stronger job than toe-nailing and eliminates the need to use "joist hangers" (these come in several different forms; see photo on page 49 for one

Diagram 1

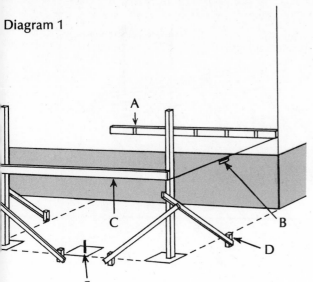

Diagram 2

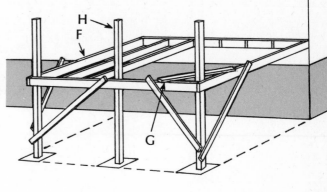

Diagram 3

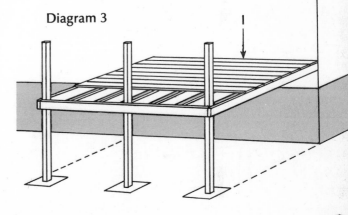

Diagram 4

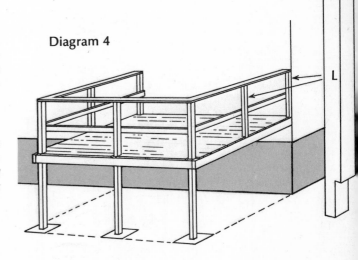

1. *With inner header nailed to house wall and joist hangers (A) nailed to it, line level (B) on taut cord is used to mark height of outer header (C) to match inner one. Diagonal supports nailed to stakes (D) hold corner posts upright. Center post is not yet in place. Bolts embedded in footings, as shown (E), fit holes in bases of posts.*

2. *With end joists (F) in place, temporary diagonal (G) keeps framing square. Center post (H) is set in place, and temporary diagonals on corner posts are rearranged, one at a time, to run from post base upward to end joists and outer header. Two intermediate joists are shown in place between the end joists. Details of frame joints are shown in Diagram B, page 48.*

3. *With all posts and joists in place, 2 × 6 decking boards (I) are nailed to joists from house outward. When about one-third of deck area is covered, structure is rigid enough to permit removal of corner diagonals and post diagonals.*

4. *In railing construction, top rail is 2 × 6. Mid-rail is 1 × 4 nailed to inside of posts. Intermediate posts (L) are notched as shown, and bolted to inside of header and end joists (gap between posts should not exceed 4 or 5 feet).*

48

Diagram A

Nails Through Header Into Joists

Temporary 2 × 4 Support

Metal Stud

This small deck frame can be assembled on the ground first, then lifted into position by two or three people.

Diagram of a typical deck frame; sections marked B, which bridge and strengthen spaces between joists, are staggered a few inches apart for more effective frame-stiffening.

Diagram B

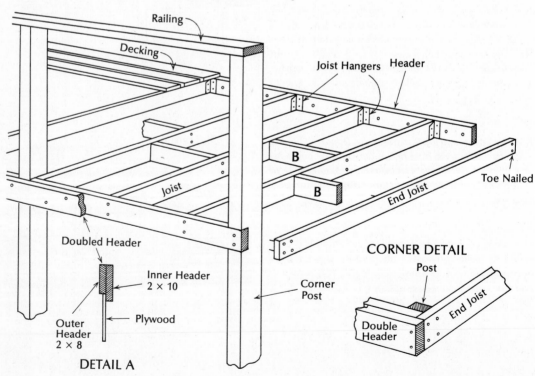

Railing

Decking

Joist Hangers

Header

B

B

Toe Nailed

Joist

End Joist

Doubled Header

Inner Header
2 × 10

Outer
Header
2 × 8

Plywood

Corner
Post

DETAIL A

CORNER DETAIL

Post

Double
Header

End Joist

example). In planning your deck, try to use joist measurements that coincide with standard lumber lengths; this will cut down dramatically on the amount of sawing to be done.

Once the deck frame has been secured to the posts, nail temporary diagonals in both directions from the frame to the base of the corner posts. Also nail a temporary diagonal across each corner of the floor frame. Then start nailing the decking boards (or plywood) to the floor frame. For 2 × 6 decking, use 3½-inch nails, two at each nailing line. For plywood, use nails three times as long as the plywood thickness. When the decking reaches the diagonals at the outer corners of the frame, the structure will be rigid enough to permit removal of the diagonals.

A typical joist hanger for use with 2 × 8 joists.

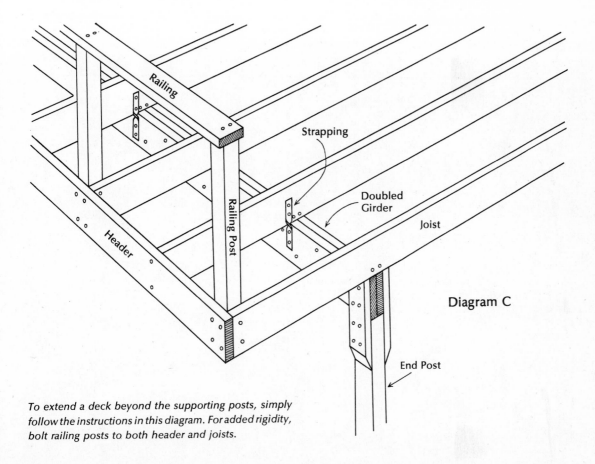

Diagram C

To extend a deck beyond the supporting posts, simply follow the instructions in this diagram. For added rigidity, bolt railing posts to both header and joists.

If you are working alone or have only one helper, your best bet is to nail the inner header to the house first. If the header is to be nailed to siding made of shingles or clapboard, be sure the nails are long enough to go through the siding and sheathing and on into the house header or end joist (a 4- or 4½-inch common nail is usually about right). Then nail joist hangers to the header at the proper spacing, preferably 16 inches from the center of one to the center of the next. Depending upon your local building code, it's possible to space them 2 feet apart, but larger joists will then be required. In that case, use common nails about 2 inches long, two on each side of the hanger.

Next, erect the corner posts, plus any intermediate posts needed to support the outer header so that it won't sag. You can brace the posts temporarily by nailing diagonals to stakes planted firmly in the ground. Then fasten the end joists in place with 1½-inch common nails (or 1-inch galvanized roofing nails) through the joist hangers at the house end. Use 4-inch nails through the outer header into the outer ends of the joists. Nailing the outer ends will be much easier at this stage if you first drill nail holes through the header. As soon as the end joists are secured, nail temporary diagonals from the joists to the base of the corner posts and from the outer header to the base of the corner posts.

From there on, it's simply a matter of adding joists between the ends. Lift each joist, lower it into a joist hanger, and nail through the header into the joist's outer end. Use 4-inch common nails, two for the

This delightful, curved deck arrangement offers both privacy and ample shade.

2×6 joists and three for the 2×8 joists. Then nail at the hangers.

After you've secured the first few joists, nail a temporary diagonal across the outer corner at one end in order to hold the corner square. If it's a trifle off square, push it into the correct position before nailing the second end of the temporary diagonal. A large carpenter's square is good for checking this. After all joists are in, nail down the decking from the house outward.

Masonry Walls

If your deck must be attached to a masonry wall—such as stone or masonry block—the best way to support it at the house–deck juncture is on masonry piers built against the masonry wall of the house as shown in the drawing below. Because these piers are cemented to the house wall, they can be built as a column of double or single blocks laid in mortar atop one another. You can buy the mortar mix packaged dry in bags. The columns, of course, should begin from concrete footings slightly larger than the column, poured in holes dug against the house foundation, and should be below the frost line. Check your local code; it may also permit you to attach the deck to the wall with masonry anchors or shields, or similar devices, thus eliminating the need for piers along the wall. If the code doesn't seem applicable to your situation, ask your building inspector for some advice.

Railings

With the method of deck construction shown in Diagram B, the supporting posts

A deck attached to a masonry wall should rest on piers, as shown, in order to support heavy loads. As an alternative, masonry fasteners or bolts can be inserted through the header directly into the house foundation.

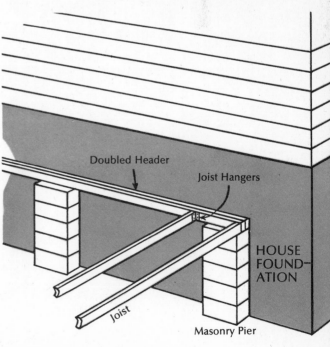

Doubled Header

Joist Hangers

Joist

Masonry Pier

HOUSE FOUNDATION

This rustic deck arrangement ties in perfectly with the original interior design of the house. Sliding glass doors lead directly to kitchen area.

The expansive deck that skirts two sides of this house includes 4 × 4 railing posts bolted to the outside of each outer header.

extend above the deck as railing posts. If a roof is to be added later, they can be extended still higher to become eventual roof supports as well as railing supports. The roof can be added the following season—if, for example, you want to build on a pay-as-you-go basis.

If the deck is to extend beyond the supporting posts—because you seek a desired effect or because of ground conditions or contour—you have a choice of other railing post arrangements, as shown in diagram C. A deck that is to double as a play area for small children should, of course, have all reachable open spaces enclosed. Inexpen-

sive snow fence mounted inside the railing (as shown at right) is one method.

The twisted wires that link together the snow fence pickets can be stapled to the railing posts with ¾-inch hammer-driven staples. The pickets should also be nailed to the horizontal rails at about an 18-inch spacing. To retain the open appearance of the railing, simply attach welded mesh fencing instead of snow fence to the inside of the railing. Welded mesh fencing, which is available in several widths suited to railing height, should be attached with the same size hammer-driven staples. Buy the "climb-proof" mesh, which, when mounted

Standard 6 × 6 posts support this simple, functional deck, made of standard lumber sizes.

Joists under the wood patio at right rest on masonry block supports placed on well drained ground and are pitched away from house.

on the railing, will have the narrow dimensions of the openings vertical so that small children can't get their feet between the wires for climbing purposes. Although the 36-inch width is usually about right for this purpose, it can be made narrower by cutting it with metal snips. (A 48-inch width is also available.) The mesh-opening sizes most suitable are 4 × 2 inches and 2 inches × 1 inch. The first dimension given is the one that runs across the width; hence the vertical dimension when the mesh is in place. The green vinyl-coated mesh—available in 50-foot and 100-foot rolls—is rustproof and is almost invisible from a distance, creating the impression of a railing that is open. If your deck is small, ask your local hardware store whether it will sell you less than a full roll of mesh.

The advantages of having an above-ground deck with a child-proof railing-fence include providing an above-ground play area that is safe from roving dogs; a dry surface; a location that is probably observable from inside the house. Such a deck must, of course, have a railing-high gate that can be securely locked at the top of the stairs leading to the ground.

About Paint and Stain

You can use either weatherproof stain or paint on your deck and railings. The stain usually requires less-frequent attention because it won't deteriorate as fast by cracking, peeling, or chipping; it also requires less application time and costs less. If you decide later that paint would be better, you can apply paint right over the stain. If you start

with paint, however, you cannot stain over it. If you do use paint, select a good deck paint; it's especially formulated for long wearing qualities.

Be sure to apply the stain or paint to the lumber *before* construction begins. This will

Typical variation possible, using basic construction plan. Here, railing posts are bolted to outside of deck header.

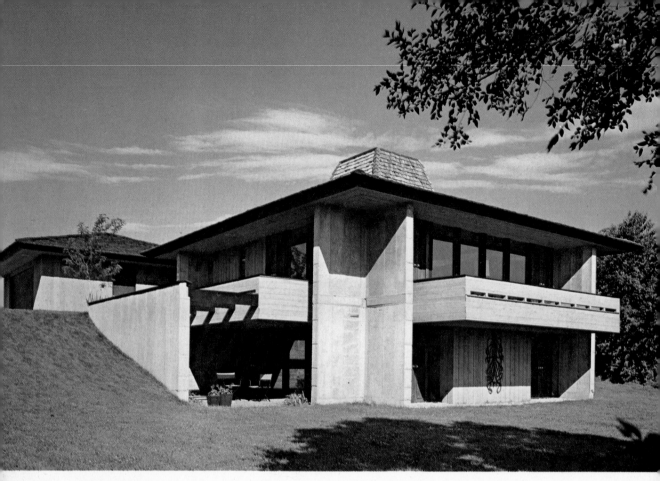

This full cantilevered deck has been tied to the house framing; deck design should therefore become an integral part of house.

eliminate the backbreaking work of painting the deck surface as well as the problem of painting the underside—especially when the deck has been built close to the ground. Painting ahead of time also ensures that all connecting wood surfaces will be protected. Parts that will be inside an enclosed storage area beneath the deck, of course, need not be painted. And any surfaces to which glue will be applied should not be painted.

Electricity

If you plan to install electric lights and outlets on your deck, it may be wise to have this done by a professional—especially if you're not familiar with electrical work. But if you have had some experience with household wiring, you'll probably find the job of wiring your deck a simple one.

Ground fault circuit protection. All outdoor plug-in receptacles, including those on decks, must now be protected by a "ground fault interrupter" (a requirement of the National Electrical Code that took effect on January 1, 1973). This device, usually referred to as a GFI, protects you from the kind of shock you might get from a tool or appliance with a faulty electrical "ground." This could be anything from a hedge trimmer to a rotisserie. If, because of broken insulation or some other trouble, electrical current reaches the outside of the tool or appliance, it becomes electrically "live." Should you touch it while standing on damp ground or while touching an iron railing or rainspout or any other "conductor" that leads to the earth, a serious or even fatal shock may result. Do not count on the fuses or circuit breakers in your house to protect you; typically, they require a load of more than 15 amperes before they break the circuit and shut off the current. But a shock of as little as 60/1000ths of one ampere can be fatal in one second. The GFI, however, responds to as little as 5/1000ths of an ampere and shuts off the current in as little as 1/40th of a second. Therefore, even though your local code may not require a GFI, it pays to include the installation of one in your deck receptacle wiring plan.

The easy way. If a single outlet is all that's needed for your deck, you can buy a GFI that mounts directly on a receptacle outlet box and connects to the regular wiring as easily as an ordinary receptacle does. Specify a weatherproof model. If you need a number of outlets, you can buy a GFI that connects into the wiring inside the house, at the fuse or breaker panel location. Wiring from this can then lead to your weatherproof deck outlets. One or the other of these types *must* be used to protect your outdoor recep-

This curved deck is actually supported by straight joists. Exterior ¼-inch plywood is curved around joist ends to give the deck its attractive appearance.

This deck built over a steep hillside requires supporting posts. Refer to the post load chart (see page 75) for correct lumber size in situations like this.

tacles if you are to follow the National Electrical Code or if your local code includes the GFI requirement. Select your GFI according to the amperage you require, usually 15 or 20 amps. (For locations protected from the weather, such as roofed porches, you can use a portable GFI and plug it into an existing outlet. This type is not weatherproof, however, and should not be left out of doors.) The code does not require a GFI in circuits that do not include outlets, such as those leading only to an outdoor post light.

Wiring to lights. If permanent post lamps are to be installed, check your local code for the type of wiring required. Code permitting, you can use type UF cable, which is buried in the earth from the house to the lights. Bury the cable at least 18 inches deep for protection, especially if it runs under any open lawn area where it might be exposed to a gardening shovel. It is easier to lead the cable out of the house through the wood framing of the house sill than to go through the masonry foundation. At the point where the cable is above ground, lead it through threaded metal conduit—a pipelike material sold by electrical suppliers—to the point where it goes below ground level. The conduit will protect it from impact damage by garden tools or mowers. Give it the same protection at any other point where it emerges from the ground—unless it is already protected by other means, such as a hollow lamp post.

The cable should be two-wire with ground, which means that it really contains three wires, one of which is the grounding

A secluded, rustic setting enhances the beauty of this deck structure set on 4 × 4 posts.

Flat or shed roofs can be extended over a deck to provide cover for a ground-level living area or an under-deck carport.

wire that attaches to the grounding terminal of receptacles or lamps. Use the wire size specified by your local code for the amperage of that circuit (the fuse or circuit breaker ampere rating). If there's no local code, use No. 14 wire for 15 amperes and No. 12 for 20 amperes. Don't worry about the durability of the cable under ground; many such installations are still in excellent condition after more than twenty years in the ground.

If your local code requires that conduit be used for all underground wiring—and some do—you can usually rent the necessary tools from a rental agency. All you need are a conduit bender and some tools for cutting and threading the conduit. The work is not as difficult as it might seem because the metal conduit is a soft alloy that bends easily.

A switch must naturally be included in the indoor portion of deck light wiring. It's also wise to include an indoor switch in the wiring to any outside receptacles. This enables you to shut off the current to the receptacles when they are not in use, thus eliminating the risk of children being injured by tampering with the outlets.

5 / PORCHES—
OUTDOOR LIVING
UNDER A ROOF

In dictionary terms, a porch is a covered entrance to a building, which projects from the wall and has its own roof. Beyond that, it may vary from being a built-on vestibule mud room all the way to being a major living area. It can be left wide open, or it can be enclosed with screening or windows to make a sun porch that is really an added room (even in the eyes of the tax assessor). Essentially, it should be built according to the way in which you plan to use it.

This traditional open porch is shielded from sun, wind, and passersby with canvas or wood roll shades. The casual furniture and comfortable surroundings reflect some of the many advantages of a porch.

The foundation is the first step in porch construction. This one, made of masonry block, starts from a concrete footing poured below the frost line.

The Floor

Check your local building code before you start your porch—especially if you plan to leave it open for a season or two and then enclose it. If it is to become a permanent room, it may have to follow a set of construction rules—from the foundation up—different from that of an open porch.

If your porch is to be at, or close to, ground level, a concrete slab floor will probably be most practical (see Chapter 3).

In general, the roof-supporting posts should rest on piers or a low wall (see illustration at left), either of which should have footings below the frost line in cold winter areas. Ideally, the masonry of the piers should extend about 8 inches above the ground, as should the post support points of a continuous wall; this will protect the wood posts from rot and ground insects. If you prefer the appearance of posts rising directly from ground level, presoak their lower ends in a rot-proofing chemical preparation. If the wall is of masonry block and terminates flush with the slab, fill the openings in the top course with concrete. You can stuff newspapers into the openings so that only the top 6 inches need be filled with concrete.

The piers or wall should be separated from the slab by an isolation joint. The reason: When the ground freezes, the slab may move slightly but the piers or wall will remain stationary because their footings are below the frost line. The isolation joint allows for this and thereby reduces the chance of cracks developing in the slab.

A typical building code is likely to require

The floor frame is secured to the top of the foundation; in this case, the floor is cantilevered 18 inches beyond the outer foundation wall.

Instead of a permanent roof, this porch is shaded by an awning, professionally tailored to fit. Ready-made types, available in sizes up to about 8 × 12 feet, can cut costs.

that footings for piers or posts have a minimum bearing area of 3 square feet (about 21 inches square) and a minimum thickness of 12 inches. For a wall built with the usual 8 × 6-inch masonry blocks, the normal requirement calls for a concrete footing 16 inches wide and 8 inches thick. If there's no code in your locality, you can follow these dimensions.

The load that your foundation can support can be estimated on the basis of soil type. Typical load-carrying capacities of soil (in tons per square foot) are as follows: soft clay, 1 ton; firm clay, 2 tons; compact fine sand, 3

When building an enclosed porch, first remove the house siding before attaching the porch wall framing to the house.

tons; loose gravel or compact coarse sand, 4 tons; and a compact sand-gravel soil, 6 tons.

If your wall is to extend high enough to support a coping around the porch, you have a choice of several construction methods. You can, of course, use masonry block alone and cap it by cementing on 8 × 16-inch patio blocks. For improved appearance, however, you may want to brick-veneer the outer surfaces (you can buy new brick that is made to simulate old brick). Or you can end the masonry block at ground level, cap it over with concrete, and continue upward with a double-thickness brick wall. Lay the bricks a course at a time, placing them side by side and filling the cracks between with mortar. For this, use a packaged mortar mix to which you need add only water.

To decide whether you need to presoak the bricks with water before laying them, test a brick selected at random from the supply at hand. Using a pencil, simply draw around a twenty-five-cent piece on the brick surface. Then, using a medicine dropper, apply twenty drops of water within the circle. If the spot stays wet for more than ninety seconds, the bricks do not need wetting. If the wet spot disappears in less than ninety seconds, spray the bricks, in batches, with a garden hose until the water runs off each individual brick. This should be done several hours before the bricks are to be laid so that the surfaces will have time to dry (wet surfaces cause the bricks to slide on the mortar). A brick wall should be reinforced by an

This porch wall has now been sheathed with plywood. A temporary scaffold permits do-it-yourselfer to work on rafters and roof decking. Here the porch roof extends partway up the house roof.

Tarpaulins are used to cover window openings in case of rain during early stages of roof work. Asphalt felt has been applied in preparation for shingling.

extra thickness at points where posts rest on it. All brick should be of type SW, which has high resistance to bad weather and freezing.

Wooden Porches

If your porch is to be far enough above ground level to allow for at least 8 inches between the framing and the ground, wooden construction is feasible (but first check the building code in your area). Typically, the framework is built like that of an open deck (see Chapter 4) except that the joists are parallel to the house wall rather than perpendicular to it. An open porch must be built in this way so that its floor can slope slightly down and away from the house for drainage. And the flooring strips (boards) must not run across the slope or water will be trapped in the tongue and groove seams. The type of flooring commonly used is called 5/4 × 4 fir flooring. (The 5/4 is a lumber term indicating the thickness of 1 5/32 inch, which is thicker than the usual interior flooring. The 4 is also a nominal term indicating less than the full 4 inches.) Ordinarily the flooring is laid directly across the joists, without a subfloor; otherwise, moisture will be trapped between the subfloor and flooring.

If the porch is to remain open, the roof should be supported by 4 × 4 posts spaced 8 feet apart, or as specified by the local building code. If it is to be enclosed, the wall construction depends on the windows to be used (see drawing on page 79 for details).

Porch windows have been installed and shingle work on the roof is in progress. Wall shingling will follow.

This porch was originally open, then later enclosed with floor-to-ceiling windows. It now serves as an added room yet retains an outdoor atmosphere. An open sun deck above would be an easy addition.

Columns topped with arches give this porch a touch of elegance without appreciable increase in building costs. The furnishings give the open porch the look and feel of indoor warmth and solidity.

This dramatic deck-porch-patio combination illustrates the advantages and relative simplicity of building your own "outdoor living rooms" with standard lumber and basic tools.

Joist size. Since joist-size requirements increase with the distance that the joists must span between supports, lumber costs for a large porch can often skyrocket. Using intermediate supports can cut these costs considerably. An intermediate foundation wall or supporting girder placed midway be-

tween the ends of a long porch, for example, will cut the joist span in half. Several such intermediate supports may be used on very long porches (see drawing below).

The roof. The simplest type of porch roof is the shed type, which is characterized by rafters perpendicular to the house wall and

To reduce the required joist size in large porch constructions, use intermediate supports (as shown) in building the foundation.

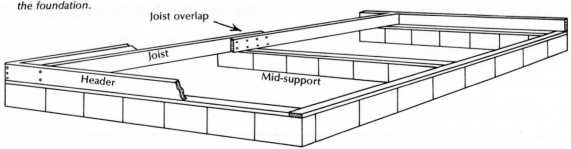

Joist overlap

Joist

Header

Mid-support

This long deck porch shows joists bolted to the headers and railings for added strength.

sloping downward away from it. They may start from a header nailed to the house wall, from the eaves of the existing roof, or from a point above the eaves of the existing roof, depending on the situation. The main considerations are appearance and the amount of headroom required under the lower end of the roof.

The easiest "decking" to apply over the rafters is exterior plywood. Use sheathing grade for economy, ½ inch thick, or whatever is required by your local code. Rafter sizes, like joist sizes, are determined by the amount of span. If there is no local code, follow the sizes in the chart on page 44. If the porch is to be an open one, no ceiling joists are necessary under the rafters. If the porch is to be enclosed, insulation should be provided; this material may be installed either above a ceiling or within the roof itself.

Shingles. These should be matched as closely as is possible to the shingles on the house roof. Lay them according to the manufacturer's instructions. Before you apply them, however, lay 15-pound asphalt felt (commonly known as tar paper) across the slope of the roof, overlapping the seams 2 inches. You can then staple the seams or fasten them with roofing nails, using only as many nails as are necessary to hold them until shingles are laid. When you apply the shingles, however, use only roofing nails with heads at least ⅜ inch in diameter.

Standard aluminum drip edge, which extends about ⅝ inch beyond deck edge, is installed over roof decking edges before shingling.

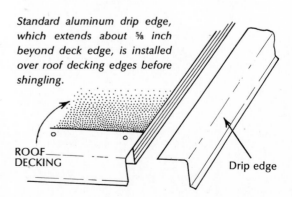

ROOF DECKING

Drip edge

If the porch is to be enclosed and heated, overlap the felt 17 inches, starting at the lower edge of the roof, and cement the overlaps (with plastic roof cement) to a point 2 feet inside the outer wall of the porch. From there on up, the overlaps need not be cemented. (Cementing the overlaps helps prevent damage from "ice dams," which form beyond the heated portion of the roof and cause trapped water to back up onto the roof and leak under the shingles.) With this system and with certain shingle types, you can pitch the roof as little as 2 inches per foot. But check with the manufacturer of the brand you intend to use before planning your roof pitch. Be sure that a preformed aluminum drip edge (see drawing on page 69) is nailed on before the roofing.

A block-styled floor and large expanse of glass create a pleasant outdoor effect in this year-round enclosed porch. Joists have been extended to form an open roof for the outdoor patio.

Louvered folding doors provide instant privacy on the enclosed porch above. Below, sliding glass doors open on to an adjacent patio. Both styles illustrate the versatility of the well-planned enclosed porch.

Heating. If the porch is to be enclosed, the heating ducts or pipes should usually be installed during the early stages of construction. If they are to run under the floor, it's easiest to put them in place before the joists are floored over. Even if the porch foundation is to be a continuous wall, ample insulation should be provided around the heating pipes or ducts. (Specify this if the heating work is to be done by a professional, which is probably the best procedure.)

If your heating system keeps the house comfortably warm during very cold weather without the burner having to operate con-

A horizontal frame member located at chair rail height reduces the chance of damage to screened or glass-enclosed porches. Wood roll-up blinds can be used for privacy when needed.

stantly, the chances are it can handle the extra load of a properly insulated porch of average size. If it must run constantly in very cold weather or if some parts of the house are chilly, electric heat may be the best answer for the porch. Initial cost is likely to be considerably lower than that of a larger main heating unit.

Wiring. The electrical wiring required for porch lighting and appliances should also be installed while the paths that the cable must follow are still accessible. The same precautions apply as described earlier for decks. If you are unfamiliar with electrical work, you'll be wise to hire a professional, but if you've had wiring experience or have a knowledge of the subject, you can save considerable expense by doing it yourself. If there is a local electrical code, be sure to obtain a copy of it. If none is available, the

National Electrical Code is an excellent guide for you to follow.

Usually, porch wiring is very simple. If the porch is to be open, use cable like type UF, which is designed for damp areas. A ground fault interrupter (GFI) must be used in conjunction with any open porch (or deck) outlets. Wiring to lights or outlets around the perimeter of the porch is best protected by leading it along the roof rafters. Portions of the wiring extending down from the rafters should be led through metal conduit or be otherwise protected. Wiring for an enclosed porch that functions as an added room is essentially the same as house wiring. Because it is not exposed to the weather, cable like Romex or BX is often used, depending on the local code. A GFI is not required, of course, except for outdoor receptacles, all of which need protection.

Screened Porches

You can make screens to fit any open porch by using "combination screen stock" molding, sometimes called simply "screen molding." This ¾ × 1¾-inch lumber has a section that has already been partially cut away, as shown in the drawing on page 74. To prepare it, sever the cutaway strip with a sharp knife or single-edged razor blade. Then, after making the screen frame, staple the edges of the screen material in the recess left by the cutaway strip. To finish the job, fasten the cutaway strip back over the stapled

A narrow roof overhang on this enclosed porch admits sunlight all year round. A wider overhang would tend to block the sunlight in summer when the sun is higher and shade is more desirable.

74

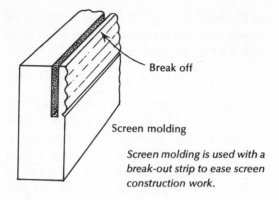

Break off

Screen molding

Screen molding is used with a break-out strip to ease screen construction work.

screening edges, using rust-proof brads or small copper nails. If you have a table saw, you can cut costs considerably by making your own screen molding from nominal 1 × 2 lumber.

If the porch posts are of straight material, such as 4 × 4 lumber, simply make the screen frames to fit snugly between them and toe-nail the frame sides to the posts. If the posts are round, fluted, or lathe-turned, it's usually simpler to mount the screens on the inside of the posts, thus eliminating the need for shaping screen members to fit.

For a feeling of openness, use a 48-inch screen width. The side frames of the screens can be stiffened by nailing them to 2 × 2 stock set behind them. This may be necessary to prevent the side frames of tall screens from bending inward. If you have pets, especially dogs, it's wise to protect the lower portion of floor-to-roof screens with an overlay of hardware cloth. This square-mesh, galvanized material is tough enough to withstand pawing. Buy a width that will reach from the floor to the height of your dog's paws, and add a nominal 1 × 2 cross frame at this point.

Vestibules
The smallest porch-building job you're likely to tackle is a built-on vestibule. Although it's an easy and relatively inexpensive addition, it can be a great convenience

when used as a miniature mud room, coat and boot room, and front-door draft eliminator.

The proper selection of windows and doors for the vestibule can avoid the "tacked-on" look. French doors or similar glazed types are a good choice. Be careful to make the structure no larger than is necessary unless you plan a full porch. The foundation (code permitting) can be made merely by pouring concrete in a trench, which has been dug below the frost line along the perimeter of the vestibule.

Masonry block or brick may then be used to bring the foundation to the necessary level. The framing of the structure can be made entirely of 2 × 4 lumber. The sheathing may be ½-inch or ⅝-inch sheathing-grade plywood, with outer siding to match the house. If the plywood is to serve as both sheathing and outer siding, it should be regular exterior grade, suitable for painting. Inside walls may be of gypsum board or paneling. It's wise to insulate walls and roof so that you can leave the front door open and enjoy either the sun or the view through the vestibule door.

Upstairs Porches
The roof of a ground-floor porch can often serve as the floor of an upper porch. Since the rafters, however, become the floor joists, they must be heavier in order to support the extra load. (Your local code will specify sizes. If there is no code, follow the chart on page 75.) The necessary degree of slope of the upper floor varies with the code, but ¼ inch per foot is widely used. In snow areas, a slope of ½ inch per foot is sometimes used to prevent water from pooling on the upper porch decking as a result of ice dams.

Exterior plywood, ⅝ inch thick, nailed over joists spaced no farther apart than 16 inches makes a satisfactory decking. It may be waterproofed in the same way as were the

This upstairs deck is supported by large columns to absorb heavy loads. Chart at bottom gives maximum post loads in thousands of pounds.

decks that have storage space under them. Or better yet, the entire area can be covered with fiber glass in regular boat-building fashion. To provide a nonskid surface, sprinkle mineral granules made for the purpose on the fresh resin used in the fiber-glassing. You can buy all the materials for the job at a marine supply outlet. Follow the instructions that accompany the brand used. The same job can be done with two-part water-phase epoxy of the type used on swimming pool decks. This material is also available in colors and can be made skidproof by using mineral granules.

Decorative Roof Posts

Posts and columns to match a wide variety of architectural styles are available on order from most lumberyards. Round columns in the southern colonial motif, for example, are available in most lengths likely to be required. The same applies to the lathe-turned posts often used on porches of houses built around the turn of the century.

Supporting posts for the porch should be sized according to their length and the load they must support. Building codes usually specify the floor load per square foot on which joist sizes must be figured. Living area floors are usually figured at a load level of 40 pounds per square foot. A habitable attic, because it is less likely to have a heavy furniture load, is often figured at 30 pounds per square foot, which is the same amount often used in planning porch framing. Thus, a 10 × 20-foot porch would call for a total load of 6,000 pounds, and its supporting posts would have to be capable of sustaining that load. The cross-sectional size (4 × 4, 6 × 6, etc.) of the posts required depends on their height. The safe loads for several of the widely used stock-lumber post sizes are

given in the chart below, but it's always a good idea to plan on a little more strength than you actually need.

Although it's worthwhile to know the reasons behind the various size requirements for the lumber you'll be using in the work you plan, you may not have to do all the figuring. In many areas, you can get the answers simply by asking the building inspector or one of his assistants for advice. The best time to do this is at a time when the building department isn't too busy.

Safe Loads for Porch Post (in thousands of pounds)

Post size	Height in feet				
	4	6	8	10	12
4 × 4	11.5	10.5	8	5	4
4 × 6	18	16	12	8	6
6 × 6	28	26.5	25	24	18

The porch or deck supported by the posts must be rigidly constructed and the posts protected from impact damage. Note that safe load decreases with height.

Once an open porch, this is now an unusually attractive living room with an open view of the outdoors on three sides. Most porches can be enclosed by the average do-it-yourselfer.

6 / HOW TO ENCLOSE YOUR DECK, PORCH, OR PATIO

One possibility to consider when you build an outdoor living area is that of enclosing it later on. If eventually you will need to add a room to your house, this may be the most economical way to go about it. And if the conversion is planned from the start, it can be a relatively simple job. If it's not planned in advance, however, a little more work may be required. In any event, unless local regulations interfere with your plans, you probably won't encounter any major problems. First, though, ask yourself whether you are certain you won't miss your outdoor living area. If it seems likely that you will, perhaps a substitute location is the answer.

A small patio was enclosed with window walls and a shed roof (right) to add a dining area to the living room below. A large header spans the section of wall that was removed.

Patio Conversions

The patio category includes any area constructed of patio block or other paving laid directly on sand. For most of us, having a sand-laid floor inside the house is not feasible, so that installing a new floor becomes part of the conversion work. If you'd like to have the same type of floor surface in your new room, however, merely lift the sand-laid paving and stack it nearby, to be used later on top of a concrete slab. If the material happens to be random-shaped flagging that required a lot of patient fitting together, take a snapshot of it before you lift it out and stack it. The snapshot can be your guide when you are placing the individual pieces back together again. You can make large numbers from stick-on tape before taking the snapshot; this will make the re-laying job as simple as working with a kit.

The sand-laid patio, therefore, poses no real conversion problem because it enables you to start from scratch. Except for the work of lifting the old paving, you begin as if the patio had never been there. And, in many instances, you may choose an altogether different base for your new room —the old patio paving can be used on a new patio if and when you decide you can't live without one.

The slab patio. If, originally, your patio was not planned for conversion, the slab is likely to be about 4 inches thick without walls or footings. If your conversion must follow a local building code, therefore, you'll probably have to build a foundation wall around the slab with footings below the frost line, as described in Chapter 3. Code permitting, however, rooms have often been built directly on the slab, without the added wall, especially in areas not subject to cold-freeze winters. Check your local requirements on this point before you get down to hard planning. If you can arrange it—and usually you can—describe the plan you have in mind to your local building inspector and ask him for suggestions. Some variation from the code may be permissible to avoid problems, and the end result may be a reduction in cost or work. In any event, you can make sure that the job you do will meet the code requirements.

The walls. The method you use to build the walls of your new room depends to a considerable extent on the size and type of windows and doors you choose. If picture

When enclosing a deck or patio, adapt conventional wall framing to desired door and window sizes. Note that doubled studs at sides of openings are arranged to support headers. Typical header sizes are listed on page 80.

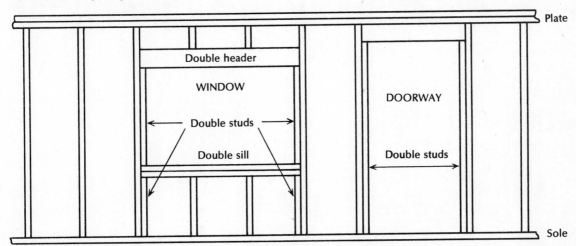

windows will account for a major portion of the wall area, the actual wall structure will consist mainly of supporting posts, with relatively little true wall. On the other hand, if you plan a more moderate window area—as in the example shown on page 79—the wall will be built of 2 × 4 studs (internal wall posts), usually spaced 16 inches apart, center to center, nailed to a 2 × 4 "sole" (lower horizontal frame member) and a doubled 2 × 4 "plate" (upper horizontal frame member). The outer skin nailed to the framework is called sheathing, and it is usually of ½-inch plywood. The drawing on page 79 of a typical wall section shows how it all goes together. The same basic assembly can be used in walls of any residential dwelling of conventional size.

Window openings. Because the supporting studs are cut away at window openings, you must place strong doubled supporting beams (called lintels or headers) across the top of the openings to take the load that would ordinarily be supported by the studs. The cross-sectional dimensions of these beams increase with the amount of span across the window opening, and are specified accordingly by most codes. If there's no code in your area, you can figure on the following typical code sizes:

Spans less than 4 feet	doubled 2 x 4's
Spans 4 to 6 feet	doubled 2 x 6's
Spans 6 to 8 feet	doubled 2 x 8's
Spans 8 to 10 feet	doubled 2 x 10's

The large posts in this expansive window wall are also supporting posts. Windows have been arranged to make the posts a part of a decorative pattern.

Notched
closure strip

Molding

Gutter

House roof

Ventilating
space

Joist hanger

30" to 38",
according to
plastic used

Outside
rafters 22"

Usual
spacing
24"

House wall

Typical roof framing used for corrugated fiberglass cover for deck or patio. Because of variations in plastic materials, follow carefully the instructions supplied with whatever brand is used.

Roof. The roof-rafter size depends on the span of the rafters and their spacing. For a given span, rafters spaced 16 inches apart can be smaller than those spaced 24 inches apart. For most spans that you are likely to encounter in porch or deck roofs, you'll be using 2 × 6's or 2 × 8's more often than other sizes. At the widely used spacing of 16 inches on centers, a typical code allows you to use 2 × 6's for spans up to 10¾ feet. If you reduce the spacing to 12 inches on centers, you can use 2 × 6's for spans up to 12½ feet. If you're using 2 × 8's at a 16-inch spacing, the span can be as much as 14 feet. At a 12-inch spacing, the span increases to 16 feet; at a 24-inch spacing, it decreases to 12 feet. Overall construction of the roof for a conversion is the same as for porches.

Deck Conversions

The procedure to follow in converting a deck to an added room is much the same as for patios. If the floor framing of the deck is lighter than that of the floors in the house, however, it should be reinforced. Otherwise, the heavier furniture loads that will be imposed on it can cause sagging or springiness. In most cases, the simplest way to reinforce the floor framing (code permitting) is by installing a girder (on posts) running at right angles to the floor joists and supporting their midpoints. Construction of the girder and posts can be similar to that shown in the section on decks with cantilevered sections (see Chapter 4). The posts should be spaced about the same as those supporting the outer header of the deck; the girder should be of the same size lumber as the outer header.

About slope. Enclosing a deck that has a slight incline in its floor (for drainage reasons) will probably not present a problem; but one with an excessive slope should be corrected as it could prove inconvenient. One way in which to do this is by jacking up the outer supports of the deck and then placing wood, metal, or troweled-in concrete shims under the bases of the posts once the deck has reached level position. This can be accomplished by using jack posts (available from building suppliers) set temporarily under the deck header. You can also solve the problem simply by nailing 4 × 4 blocks to the lower portion of the deck posts at a height that will permit the use of an automobile jack. Set the jack on top of the footing and then raise the deck to the desired position. Since the deck posts must be raised a total of only an inch or so, you can often raise one or two posts at a time. Watch the header carefully, however, for signs of stress. Usually, the safest procedure is to raise each post a fraction of the total required amount and then elevate the others successively by the same amount. This is less likely to cause excessive bending of the header, and it will enable you to finish the job in only two or three stages of jacking.

About Floors

Whether you are enclosing a patio or a deck, you need a floor that is suitable for an inside room of your home, as opposed to one for an outdoor living area. As we've noted, the surface might be of flagstone or brick in cases where a slab patio is involved. But if your house has hardwood flooring throughout, you will probably want your new room to match—and there's no reason why it can't. If the converted area is to be a family room, of course, you may prefer resilient flooring of the types widely used in basement family rooms. Asphalt tile or vinyl asbestos tile, for example, can be applied directly to a concrete floor. You can also use rubber-backed carpet, indoor-outdoor carpet, or most other similar types placed over a suitable pad. (Your carpet dealer can specify the type of pad best suited to over-slab use for the carpeting you select.)

Hardwood flooring on a slab. Assuming that there is no moisture problem, you can choose any one of several methods to lay

When building a slab patio that is to be enclosed later on, pour concrete on a polyethylene layer. Use an upper layer of same material, as shown, under hardwood floor.

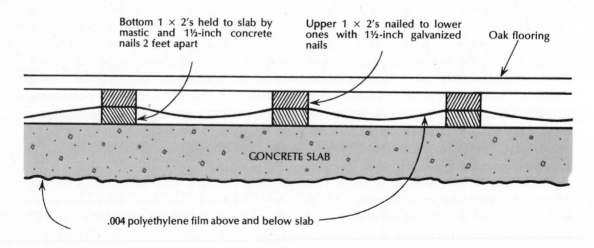

Bottom 1 × 2's held to slab by mastic and 1½-inch concrete nails 2 feet apart

Upper 1 × 2's nailed to lower ones with 1½-inch galvanized nails

Oak flooring

CONCRETE SLAB

.004 polyethylene film above and below slab

The home handyman at right is laying down strips of mastic prior to covering slab with polyethylene sheets.

hardwood flooring over a slab. If you prefer the traditional strip flooring, the first step is to apply a moistrue barrier of polyethylene sheet (use the standard thickness of .004 inch) to the surface of the slab. The proper adhesive is a "cut back" asphalt mastic formulated specifically for flooring use.

The polyethylene sheet is smoothed onto the fresh mastic after the latter has been spread over the concrete. Try for good, overall contact. Then coat the undersides of the 2 × 4 "sleepers" (see diagram below) with the same mastic, and bed them down on the polyethylene as shown. Lock them in place with masonry nails driven through the sleepers and into the concrete. Buy the masonry nails from your building supply dealer; to make certain there won't be any mistake about the length, tell him that the nails must go through 2 × 4's into concrete. The sleepers are laid in a staggered pattern, as shown, to allow for the circulation of air under the wood floor. An alternate method is to use 1 × 2's nailed one on top of the other as shown on pages 82 and 84–85.

Nailing the flooring. After the sleepers are in place, "blind-nail" the flooring strips across them at right angles. To do this, you'll need a special nailing tool that can usually be borrowed or rented from your flooring supplier. These tools vary in design, but they all do the same job. Typically, the tool holds a supply of flooring nails so that the nail to be driven is set at the correct angle for driving through the edge of the flooring strip. The nails, which are also designed especially for flooring use, are driven through the tongued edge of each flooring strip so that the groove of the next strip conceals them. Ask for instructions in the use of the nailing tool when you get it; if you've had any experience with

Staggered 2 × 4 sleepers, fastened to slab over polyethylene with mastic and masonry nails, are used to form a wood flooring base over concrete.

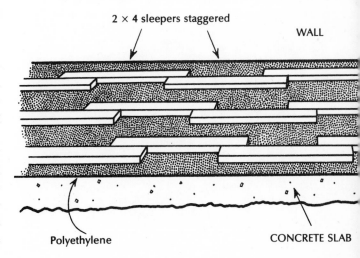

2 × 4 sleepers staggered

WALL

Polyethylene

CONCRETE SLAB

A strip of 1 × 2 is beaded in mastic and nailed to slab with masonry nails.

woodworking tools, however, you should have no trouble with this one. Otherwise, it might be prudent to have your flooring installed by a professional.

Start the flooring strips with the grooved edge of the first one about ⅝ inch from the wall and with the tongued edge on the outside for nailing. The edge next to the wall should be nailed in conventional fashion, down through the surface into the sleepers. The baseboard or shoe molding will conceal the nailheads. The ⅝-inch gap between the first flooring strip and the wall allows for expansion of the flooring. It may be increased to 1 inch if the combined thickness of the baseboard and shoe molding are enough to cover it. Leave a similar gap when you reach the other side of the floor; you'll probably have to saw the final strip to proper width for this purpose. If you have a portable circular saw (the usual builder's type), simply set the guide fence to the width you want and make the cut.

For this job, use "end-matched" flooring, whereby each piece has one end grooved and the other end tongued (like the edges), so that the end joints are locked solidly to ensure a smooth overall surface. Because flooring is usually sold in random lengths, it might be advisable to lay the strips side by side before you begin the nailing so that you can arrange the end joints in a staggered pattern. Make sure that the end joints in adjoining strips do not meet each other.

Finishing. If you are installing unfinished flooring, it will be necessary to sand the floor area after the work is complete. You can rent a floor sander and an edge sander (for sanding close to walls) from your flooring sup-

Polyethylene sheet is laid over lower 1 × 2 strips and fastened in place by nailing on upper 1 × 2 strips.

Polyethylene sheets are overlapped at seams before final strips are nailed in place.

plier or tool rental agency. Find out how to use the sanders when you arrange to rent them; they are not difficult to operate, but you must remember to keep them moving. A powerful floor sander left running in one spot will quickly grind a deep furrow into your floor surface.

Use any good floor finish and follow the manufacturer's instructions. Polyurethane types are popular because of their toughness—which is important in areas where heavy traffic is expected. Since timing between coats is important with this type, follow the instructions closely.

Penetrating resin finishes are also widely used on flooring, and they claim advantages of their own. In general, they are applied liberally, allowed to soak in for a period of time specified by the manufacturer, and then wiped off completely. The material hardens in the cells of the wood, after which wax can be applied for added luster. If later on a heavy traffic area becomes worn, you merely remove the wax from the worn area (with a wax solvent purchased from your paint supplier) and recoat the area with the penetrating resin finish. After it has hardened, simply rewax the area and you will find that it will blend without any patched effect. Localized wear, therefore, does not require overall refinishing—which is one good reason for penetrating resin floor finishes having become so popular.

Whatever type of finish you use, follow the manufacturer's instructions. Even among finishes of the same basic type, different brands may vary greatly in formula and length of hardening time.

Prefinished flooring, of course, requires

Rent or borrow a floor nailing machine to finish blind-nailing of flooring.

Flooring is nailed through tongued edge to conceal nail heads when the job is completed.

resilient flooring (or resilient tiles), you'll do better with ½-inch plywood. All plywood seams that run parallel to the decking strips should be located right on the decking strips—not on the gap between strips. From the subfloor on, the flooring procedures are the same as for any other room in the house.

Insulation. If the deck being enclosed is supported on piers and the space under it will not be enclosed, the floor should be insulated. This may be done easily by bonding rigid foam insulation to the underside of the decking strips, between joists, using a mastic made for this purpose. Or you can use conventional fiber-glass insulation, stapled in place. For added warmth at floor level, cover the underside of the floor framing with weather-resistant insulating board. (This job will be much easier if you have a helper to hold the panel in place while you do the nailing.)

Porch Conversions

A roofed porch is usually the simplest type of conversion job because a major portion of the room structure has already been completed. In general, the conversion is simply a matter of closing the space between posts and of installing windows. The slope of the porch floor, which is a normal requirement for drainage purposes, can be corrected in most cases by one of the methods mentioned previously. If the incline is slight, however, you may not find it worth the trouble to correct.

Heating. To minimize the heating requirements of your new indoor room, use the thickest insulation you can fit between inner and outer walls and repeat the process for the roof. If the room calls for a level ceiling below the rafters, install the insulation on top of the ceiling, between the ceil-

no sanding or finishing; be sure, however, that the room is thoroughly dried out before you install the flooring. If you use prefinished flooring squares (somewhat similar in effect to parquet), the squares may be laid directly on the moisture-sealed slab with mastic made for the purpose.

Deck flooring. If you are enclosing a deck that is floored with the usual deck strips of 2 × 6 or 2 × 4, with intervening gaps, a subfloor of plywood must go over it. As a first step, lay 15-pound asphalt felt at right angles across the deck strips, allowing a 2- to 3-inch overlap at the seams. Then lay the plywood subfloor. If you plan to use hardwood strip flooring and if the flooring strips will be nailed through the plywood directly into the boards, you can cut costs considerably by using ⅜-inch-thick plywood instead of ½ inch or more. If you are planning to use

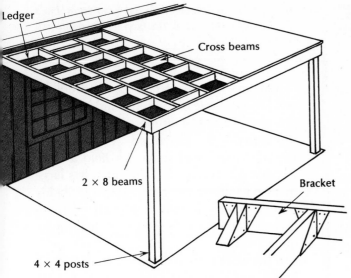

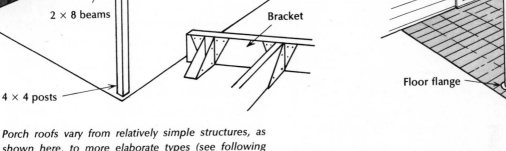

Ledger

Cross beams

2 × 8 beams

Bracket

4 × 4 posts

2 × 4 ledger

2" pipe

Elbow

Floor flange

Porch roofs vary from relatively simple structures, as shown here, to more elaborate types (see following pages). Roof material can range from aluminum and plywood to fiber glass or aluminum.

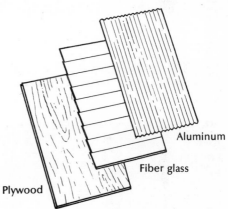

Aluminum

Fiber glass

Plywood

ing joists. If the ceiling is to be a sloping one fastened to the underside of the roof rafters, use the thickest insulation that will fit the space. If your rafters are 2 × 6's, use 6-inch fiber-glass insulation; it will fit the space even though 2 × 6's actually measure only 1½ × 5½ inches.

If your present central heating unit can't handle the addition—it may already be operating at full capacity in very cold weather—electric heat in the new room may be the simplest answer. Check with your local power company about special rates for electric heating. If you don't know of an electrician, the power company may be able to suggest one. *Do not try to install your own electric heating unit unless you are familiar with house wiring.*

Typically, electric heating units are of the baseboard type, operating on 240 volts. The wiring is led directly from the fuse, or circuit breaker panel, through a double-pole, single-throw thermostat to the units. The circuit is, of course, a grounded type.

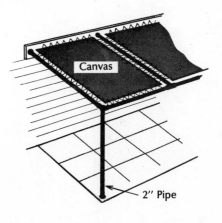

Canvas

2" Pipe

The small enclosed porch (left) has been transformed into a bright breakfast nook. Doors on either side provide easy access to patio.

Just how much wattage is required depends on the size of the room and its insulation. In a 12 × 14-foot room with maximum insulation, as described earlier, two 750-watt baseboard units can hold a comfortable temperature. If the room has large picture windows, however, it will probably require more wattage (although double-glass windows will help reduce heating requirements).

If the work is to be done by a professional, he will undoubtedly be able to estimate with considerable accuracy the size of the heating units needed. He will also know, of course, the code requirements.

Nature can play a role in solving your heating needs, too. If the enclosed porch has a south wall, for example, a large double-glass window area on that side can play an important part in heating the room during the daytime hours. A proper roof overhang will automatically block the same sun in the summertime when its heat is not desirable.

Conversion Tips

If you are enclosing a slab patio, the floor will be warmer if the perimeter of the slab is insulated from the outside ground with foam, made for in-ground use. Your building supplier can order the correct type of foam for this purpose. If you lay a slab for a patio that you plan to enclose at a later date, place a polyethylene moisture barrier on top of the base on which the slab is to be laid before the concrete is formed. This will provide maximum protection later when you lay a

This dressing room (left) was converted from a slab patio. Electricity and heat were installed at start of job.

This spacious porch (right) began as an open patio. Now custom-built screens or glass windows have converted the structure into year-round use.

wooden floor over the slab. A moisture barrier on top of the slab (beneath the flooring) should also be used.

If your conversion involves a deck that rests on piers too close to the ground to allow for working below it, insulating the floor is obviously not the solution. The best answer to this problem is to close the space between piers. This can be done either by building a masonry wall between the piers, with its footings set at the same depth (as the piers), or by means of a lightweight curtain wall.

This converted porch, similar to the one above, makes ideal use of 4 × 4 posts and screening to bring outdoor and indoor living together.

The method you use to build the latter type of wall depends on the dimensions of the area it must cover. In some instances, such walls are made of plywood with aluminum flashing serving as a connecting strip to the ground. Or, if the deck is very low, the flashing alone may be used. Asbestos cement board is another readily available material sometimes used. Important: In whatever way the wall is built, it should allow for freeze-heaving.

Vents

No matter which method is used to enclose the underdeck space, a few screened vent openings are essential for proper air circulation. Without such vents, the enclosed space under a low deck or porch will become excessively damp and eventually lead to wood rot. In cold climates, you can install factory-built vents with hinged covers that can be closed in winter. If possible, install at the same time a larger, unvented, hinged opening to be used strictly for inspection purposes.

Insect Protection

If your area has a history of termite or carpenter ant problems, be sure to take protective measures against them. If you have plans to build a continuous foundation wall to enclose the underdeck space, it would be wise to cap it with a termite shield of aluminum flashing. This is simply a continuous strip of flashing cemented to the top of the wall and protruding 2 inches beyond the inside of the wall. The protruding portion is bent downward at an angle of 45 degrees. It's usually possible to set this strip in place, already bent, and cement it from the outside. If indeed wood-attacking insects are common to your area, it becomes especially important to add the inspection opening mentioned earlier; this will allow room to

This simple porch arrangement is ideal for conversion purposes. It also blends in perfectly with the architectural style of the house itself.

Here a porch roof has been utilized to maximum advantage. Entry doors on the second-floor level afford easy access to sun deck.

spray under the deck from time to time. Chlordane is an extremely effective agent to use against most kinds of destructive ants and termites.

Chlordane can also be used to create a barrier in the soil through which termites cannot possibly travel without suffering exposure and death. This can be done by digging a narrow trench in the ground around the foundation, mixing chlordane with the soil you've removed, and then filling in the trench with the treated dirt. To do this properly, follow the directions on the chlordane container.

Instant Patios

Suppose you have completed your conversion job and you discover that your sheltered outdoor living area was indispensable after all. You can have it back, space permitting, with very little effort. Just buy enough gravel to cover a 10×20-foot area, and put a roof over it with the aid of a ready-made kit that comes complete with supporting posts and instructions. All you have to do is bolt it together. Usually made of aluminum, these patio covers are available at many lumberyards and building suppliers or they can be purchased from mail-order houses. The price varies with the snow load that the roof must carry; this is often figured on the basis of 20 pounds for light snow areas, 40 pounds for moderate, and 60 pounds for heavy snow areas. You may purchase accordingly.

If you can't find a patio cover in keeping with the style of your house, you may be able to extend the overhang of your conversion and cover it with translucent fiber-glass panels, as shown on page 81. Be sure to plan on a pitch of 1 inch per foot or more.

7 / OUTDOOR LIVING EQUIPMENT

Once your outdoor living area is completed, you'll begin shopping for the things that will help make it the fun place you want it to be. You'll need outdoor furniture, cooking equipment, possibly a game or two—and for a final touch, something to provide the kind of background music you and your friends can enjoy with outdoor living. And still, you want it all to be as convenient and trouble-free as possible.

This free-standing awning creates a festive tent effect while it shields the patio table from sun, sudden showers, and falling leaves.

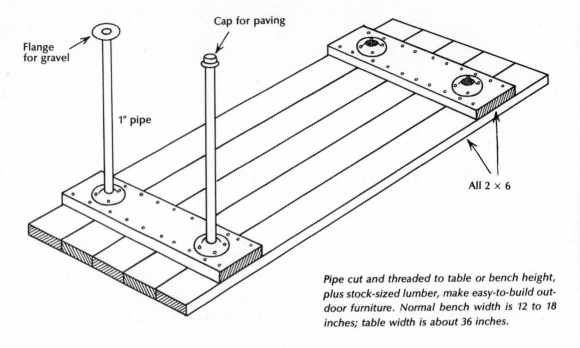

Flange
for gravel

Cap for paving

1" pipe

All 2 × 6

Pipe cut and threaded to table or bench height, plus stock-sized lumber, make easy-to-build outdoor furniture. Normal bench width is 12 to 18 inches; table width is about 36 inches.

Furniture

It is assumed that you will select your furniture according to your own taste and the decorative scheme you have in mind (see Chapter 8). You'll also want it to be both economical and durable. If your choice is wooden furniture, think about making it yourself. Some of the most attractive, most popular styles are the simplest to build —and you can custom-build them to suit the space in which they will actually be used.

Ready-made pieces, on the other hand, are frequently too big or too small for the space available. But if you don't enjoy doing-it-yourself or if you simply lack the time for it, shop carefully and you'll probably find furniture to fit. If you do decide to build your own furniture, however, the drawing above illustrates a simple type of bench and table construction that can be easily adapted to almost any available space. If you're reasonably handy with tools, you'll also find it a simple matter to copy a style to which you've taken a fancy. Most wooden furniture styles are easy to duplicate with average home shop tools. But whether you buy or build wooden outdoor furniture, it's advisable to choose a folding type that can be winter-stored under protective shelter. Otherwise, rainwater will seep between the joined parts and cause freezing and loosening of joints.

This low table is made from stock framing lumber, using 4 × 4 stubs for legs.

This rustic setting is enhanced by a combination deck and patio flooring, using existing trees and plantings to ensure privacy. The simple lounge furniture complements the arrangement.

What about the possibility of wood rot? This can be a common problem, but it is not likely to occur on a paved patio or a deck. Certain woods, like redwood, have a high degree of rot resistance, and most other widely used species can also withstand years of weathering without trouble. In case you happen to acquire some aging wooden lawn furniture that already has rotted areas, however, there is on the market an easy remedy. Two-part marine preparations can actually make rotted areas harder and tougher than

new wood. In general, they are liquid forms of epoxy and other resins that soak into the pores of the rotted area, which is naturally more absorbent than sound wood. When this material hardens (overnight usually), it literally turns the rotted wood into a hard, tough plastic that cannot rot. You can use the same material on rotted parts of decks, porches, facia boards, and trim. You can even use it inside the house where plumbing that sweats or leaks has caused flooring to rot (frequently around showers and toilet

bowls). Wherever you use this liquid resin, be sure that the rotted area is completely dry before you apply it. You can buy the resin at large boatyards and marine supply dealers. Explain to them that you are looking for a preparation that hardens rotted wood. A number of brands are available, and they have saved yacht owners many thousands of dollars on repairs.

Aluminum furniture requires little care. The webbing commonly used for seats and backs eventually needs replacing, but you can buy this material in rolls or kits, usually from the same source as the furniture itself. Iron and steel furniture is also easy to maintain—simply make it a point to touch up any chipped or rusted spots as soon as they occur; if neglected, rust tends to spread to the painted areas adjacent to the trouble spot. Use a wire brush or fine sandpaper to remove rust or loose paint. On ornate cast-iron furniture, the wire brush is probably the best choice because it works its way into grooves and fissures. Follow up with one of the rust-resistant paints—but be sure to read the directions on the can before you start. If a primer is required, apply it as directed before adding the finish coat. If the rust-resistant paint doesn't come in the furniture color, you can use a final coat of any good oil-base outdoor gloss enamel that matches the furniture color.

For gravel patios, choose furniture that has ample surface areas on the base of the legs because small leg tips tend to sink into the gravel. Look for metal furniture with metal disks on the leg tips. If you can't find

Light, iron-framed chairs and glass-topped table to match make a good choice for a small patio. Similar designs are available in aluminum.

Rattan furniture is a particularly good choice when it is protected from inclement weather by an overhead roof.

Redwood is by far the most popular wood for outdoor furniture because of its color and resistance to wood rot. Here it is used generously and effectively on this modest but functional patio.

this type, try to match rubber crutch tips (usually available at hardware and dime stores) to the leg ends. If you can't find a matching size, buy the next larger size and use electrical tape wrapped around the leg tips to make up the difference. Rubber tips are also recommended for paved patios and decks because they will reduce the abrasion and noise of sliding chairs on your patio or deck surface.

Cookout Equipment

Equipment for outdoor cooking may range all the way from a simple charcoal grill to a

This angled patio bench, made of 2 × 4s with short 1 × 4 spacers, rests on 4 × 4 legs. Chairs on opposite page are molded plastic.

gas-fired brazier or to a combination of units that includes an electric broiler-oven or a rotisserie. If you plan to include electrical equipment, proper outlets must be provided, of course, with sufficient wattage to operate these units. You'll find the wattage on the specification plate of the equipment. If you're unfamiliar with wiring, hiring an electrician is your best bet. Some sound advice: Have the outlets protected by a ground fault interrupter (GFI), or purchase a plug-in type of GFI that can be used in other outlets when necessary. Whatever outdoor electrical equipment you use should, of course, be brought inside or otherwise protected from the weather when not in use.

Charcoal grills. The fastest way to get your outdoor living underway is to buy an inexpensive charcoal grill—which you can usually do for less than the price of a good-sized steak. If your plans call for a lavish masonry grill unit later on, use the inexpensive model for your cookouts until you're ready to tackle the big job.

One of the easiest ways to build a barbecue is with $8 \times 8 \times 16$-inch masonry blocks, as shown in the drawing. Or, following the same general plan, you can build one with brick almost as easily. Even better is a grill constructed of natural stone dug from your own soil—at no cost. If you like the idea of stone but your lawn doesn't have an adequate supply, you can also buy it.

It's important, if you build with stones that come from the soil, however, to wash them clean before starting the cement work. The easiest way to handle the job is with a packaged mortar mix. For building a grill *without* mortar, masonry-block kits are available from most masonry suppliers. The

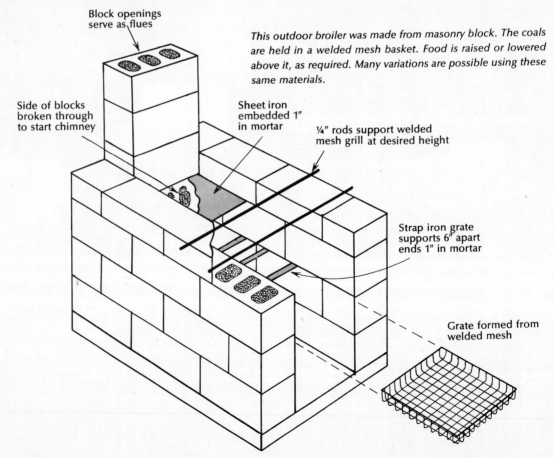

Block openings serve as flues

This outdoor broiler was made from masonry block. The coals are held in a welded mesh basket. Food is raised or lowered above it, as required. Many variations are possible using these same materials.

Side of blocks broken through to start chimney

Sheet iron embedded 1" in mortar

¼" rods support welded mesh grill at desired height

Strap iron grate supports 6" apart ends 1" in mortar

Grate formed from welded mesh

For a luxury patio, cooking facilities made of brick are often desirable. Plan brickwork around the grill units and build accordingly.

blocks fit together dry, with locking joints, and take a metal grill that fits the completed unit. It looks like a permanent piece of masonry, but you can take it apart and set it up elsewhere; this feature will come in handy if you have to move later on.

About charcoal. To achieve a fast, hot flame in your grill, look for a source of *plain charcoal*, which is usually recognizable by its irregular shape (often that of a small piece of log or branch). It starts quickly, and while it doesn't last as long as the regular briquets,

most afficionados of seared steaks prefer it. Good briquets can also sear your steak appetizingly, of course, but you must allow more cooking time. Perhaps the best compromise is to use briquets for your cookouts and keep a reserve of regular charcoal for the seared-meat purists. To attain maximum cooking control with either type of charcoal, select a unit whose grill can be easily raised and lowered. If you plan to do any pan cooking over charcoal, try a hibachi as auxiliary equipment. Once you have the knack of

A privacy fence and natural greenery rim this patio in close quarters; bench is supported by steel legs. The floor-level charcoal grill features this colorful site.

Ready-made, colorful cushions and backrests highlight this built-in curved patio bench and sunken grill.

using these units, you'll find that their draft adjusters provide good control at relatively low cooking temperatures.

To avoid fire hazards on those occasions when a grill must be left with its coals still burning, be sure to cover the grill with a metal cover. It will keep wind gusts from scattering sparks and protect the brazier from rain, which can turn the ashes into instant slush. Simple round braziers can be neatly covered with a metal trash-can lid.

An easy way to make your own cover is to cut a large disk (several inches larger than the round brazier) with a pair of tin snips from a sheet of aluminum (available at most hardware stores) or from a galvanized sheet (sold by plumbing suppliers). Then cut inward from the perimeter to the center of the disk and form the metal into a cone by over-

lapping the edges of the cut. The completed cover should have the general shape of a coolie hat. To hold the overlapped seams together, you can use small nuts and bolts or pop rivets.

Gas grills. These units can be used with natural gas or bottled gas, but be sure they are equipped for whichever type you choose. (Conversion kits are made for most models.) A typical tank-type gas grill will operate for about twenty-five cooking hours on a 20-pound tank of gas, so you're likely to obtain a full season's use of the grill from a single tank. When the tank is empty, simply take it back to your supplier for a refill. (You can tell when the tank is nearing the refill point by noting the total weight when it is full—printed on the tank—and then weighing the used tank on your bathroom scale.)

If your kitchen range also operates on bottled gas, you can eliminate the need for a separate tank by connecting the grill into the supply line from the main tank. This tank is usually a larger one, permanently installed, and is kept filled by your gas supplier. A word of caution: Work on gas lines must be done properly for safety's sake. Your local code may require that it be done by a licensed plumber; in any event, don't tackle the job yourself unless you are absolutely sure you can do it right.

Grills are made in both fixed and portable types. A fixed grill is usually mounted on a hollow metal post, with one end inserted about 2 feet into the ground. A gas-supply pipe runs underground to the grill and up through the post into the burner. The portable grill is mounted on a flat base, sometimes called a patio base (which in some models moves on rubber-tired wheels). A flexible gas-supply hose connects the grill to the supply pipe or to the small supply tank; this allows you to move the grill in a radius of about 12 feet.

If you want to use your grill all year round, as many people do, weatherproof models are available. That way, you can broil a steak outdoors in the dead of winter and bring it inside for dinner. The charcoal taste is thereby acquired without smoking up the kitchen—and you won't have any broiler pans to clean.

Music

To avoid moving a record player or similar equipment back and forth between the house and the outdoors, try this easy method to bring music to your deck, porch, or patio: Mount a weatherproof speaker (use two for stereo) close to your outdoor living area, and make the necessary connections to the record player in the house. If you're not familiar with the workings of hi-fi and stereo equipment, check with your local dealer about the necessary accessories.

The simplest arrangement is to have cords leading to the speakers that enable you to disconnect the indoor speakers and connect the outside ones without moving the turntable itself. You need to know the distance from your unit to the outdoor speakers, of course, so that the hookup can be made correctly. One important precaution with this type of indoor–outdoor speaker system is never to turn on the unit unless at least one pair of speakers is connected to it. Turning on the player without speakers connected can cause serious damage to the unit. To avoid this possibility, have your serviceman connect the speakers through a selector switch box so that when you switch off one pair of speakers, you automatically switch on the other (if you would like music playing inside and outside at the same time, ask your serviceman to set it up for you).

Outdoor speakers are easy to mount on the wall of the house, on posts, or even on trees. Be sure all connecting lines are located so that they aren't in the way of people or animals moving about them. Connecting wires can be led through a hole bored in the house wall, with a short piece of plastic pipe pushed through the hole to serve as a lining (pick a pipe diameter big enough for the cables). After the cables are led through the pipe, seal the outer end with electrician's sealing putty. Mounting straps or staples will secure the wiring to the house walls where the connections are made.

The gas-fired grill (opposite) is permanently mounted for use at any time of year, weather permitting. Broil your steaks outside, and serve them inside for year-round, charcoal-broiled pleasure.

8 / BE YOUR OWN OUTDOOR DECORATOR

Once you have finished building the family's outdoor living area, it's time to add the fancy trimmings to your handiwork.

With the outdoor world of nature for a backdrop, decorating your deck, patio, or porch (open or closed) is more fun than work. It is indeed a creative challenge. Here you have no worries about what goes with what—you can use any color in the spectrum so long as it doesn't clash with the exterior siding of your house. But you can give even that the natural look by using vines and a profusion of tubs and other containers of flowering plants. It stands to reason that you like the color of your house or you wouldn't have chosen it in the first place, so don't let it limit your imagination.

Nature provides the major part of the decor that complements this table setting. The patterned glass tabletop reflects foliage and sky hues. Wrought iron furniture, though delicate in appearance, is a wise choice for durability.

The dramatic arrangement above features contemporary fireplace and furnishings in a timeless setting.

Tie indoor and outdoor areas together. Extending a dominant color from the room adjacent to your patio or deck to the outside area is the simplest way to "put it all together." If the room has a solid-color carpet, the deck or porch floor can be matched with an indoor-outdoor carpet to unite visually the two areas. Using a matching paint or stain on the outdoor floor can also do the trick inexpensively. (Stain comes in almost as many basic colors as paint.) Or perhaps there is an accent color in the room—for example, a tablecloth—that can be used for the outdoor chair cushions. Another easy way to capture a color from the room and use

it outside is to paint the wood or metal frames of your outdoor furniture in the same color, using a high-gloss enamel, which is easy to clean and creates a smart, high-style effect.

Emphasize the difference. If, on the other hand, you want to create a dramatic change of scene, disregard the interior and go all-out with new colors and an entirely different style of furniture and accessories. For example, stepping from the subdued atmosphere of a formal, period living room onto a deck or patio that is done in brilliant, contemporary colors and furniture forms— perhaps with a jungle aura about it—can create a distinct change of mood that can give a lift to summertime outdoor living. If the area is not sunny enough for flowering plants to thrive, use greens in hot-hued pots and tubs. Or build your own planters and improvise trellises and supports for climbing varieties. And don't overlook the possibilities of using some of the new artificial blooms.

About Color
In good decorating—inside or out—color is your most versatile, dependable tool. It will work just as hard for you outside your home as it does inside. It can shove walls away from you in a small room and make that room seem larger, or it can cause bulky but useful pieces of furniture to all but disappear into the background. Color can emphasize the importance of a treasured piece so that its presence cannot be denied. Light colors —such as yellow and white—will reflect light and heat away. Dark colors absorb and trap heat.

Cut flowers and colorful furniture enhance the sparkle of this porch bar that looks out on the adjacent patio. The effect of drapes behind porch posts adds interest.

Add color to a patio corner bench by rimming it with flower boxes. Build the boxes around ready-made plastic flower troughs, to reduce chance of wood rot.

Cast flower boxes of masonry in the size and shape required, or use standard masonry blocks, and plant flowers in the hollow core sections.

If your deck is a small, built-on addition to your home, make it appear more spacious than it really is by judicious use of your favorite colors. Light tones tend to blend into their background; thus, a pale tone for both floor and railing will lead the eye outward toward your landscape. The less broken up your color scheme is, the more effective your small outdoor living area will seem. You can attract the eye away from a small deck still farther by installing a bird feeder in a tree a short distance away from the actual living area. This will help to create a feeling of spaciousness—although it is still the overall effect that counts!

If the area is subject to direct sunlight for most of the day, cool colors—including blues, violets, and nature's own summer green—seem to cool the atmosphere. A

The triangular openings that were created when these patio slabs were poured provide a dramatic outline for flowers.

Vivid, bold, warm colors dramatically enhance this inviting porch.

An umbrella table (right) adds both shade and color to a patio that is fenced for privacy. Choose your umbrella according to the colors that surround it.

word of caution, however: If you use blues, violets, or greens on seating cushions, use them in the lighter shades because (1) they will absorb the sun's heat and become extremely uncomfortable to sit on and (2) they have an unfortunate tendency to fade in sunlight—especially the blues. However, strong, dark shades of these colors can be used as accent colors in materials that do not fade, such as ceramics found in table settings or in containers for flowers or in the painted framework of the furniture and the deck itself.

Furniture designed to complement this type of sunny area—where a roof or awning is impractical because, for example, it carries shade into the house during winter months when the sun's warmth is preferable —can solve the problem. All you have to do is follow a few basic color rules. Buying an umbrella for your table is a wise and long-lasting investment. Available in a multitude of fabrics and designs, they are more than decorative—you can tilt them against the sun at a touch; they will protect you from sudden showers, which can be disastrous to a table laden with food; or they can act as a welcome wind shield. You can indulge in any color combination that goes with your decor, but keep one cardinal rule in mind: Keep the bright colors on the underside— where you and your guests can enjoy them —but leave the outer side (i.e., the upside) white, or at least as light a shade as you can live with, so that the sun's rays are reflected away from you.

Since a shaded, cool outdoor area is likely to be chilly at times, it is advisable to plan for a reverse color scheme as well. Warm vibrant hues of yellow, orange, and red, plus all their intermediate shades, will create a glowing effect. And careful use of a sharp green or brilliant blue can point up the hot colors of the general scheme. Generous use

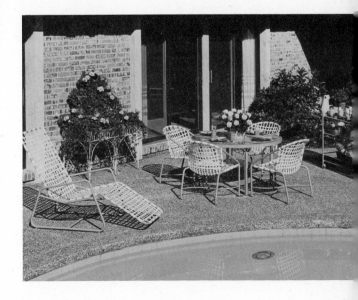

Use colorful fruit to enhance the effect of outdoor table settings, as at left. Open webbing on poolside furniture (right) is both colorful and practical.

Brickwork combines with natural surroundings to create a dramatic setting for this Spanish-type outdoor dining area.

of lights and lanterns designed for outdoor use (see page 119) will carry this feeling of warmth over into the evening hours, as will a glowing brazier for cooking and heating. A windbreak to offset the chill from prevailing breezes will also help in this situation; if a natural shield of trees and shrubs is not feasible, fencing may be the answer. Ready-made types are available at lumberyards and builder's suppliers, or you can make your own to fit your special situation and decor.

Outdoor Furniture

Furniture for use out-of-doors on a deck or patio requires more than style and comfort to recommend it. It should have weather-proof construction, such as the old reliable, comfortable redwood, which demands that

only its cushions and lounge pads be protected. The availability of replacement cushions to update the basic pieces makes this a sound investment until the time comes for a complete re-do.

In areas where showers are brief, far between, and followed by a quick, drying sun, more latitude in choice of furniture is possible. Of course, any furniture that is protected by an umbrella is weather-safe—but here's a good tip: When bad weather threatens, tilt your outdoor chairs in against the edge of the umbrella table so that the rain and wind dust will slide off the backs of the chairs. The seats will be automatically protected by the table top, which will in turn be covered by the umbrella.

Metal furniture made with a mesh surface is also a good choice—provided that the finish is weatherproof, of course. Rain simply washes through the surface of this type and becomes an added bonus in keeping your furnishings clean and fresh. It is also surprisingly easy to repaint, so that changing colors for a new decor presents no problems.

Furniture for lounging in sun or shade. Hammocks present a beguiling promise on a summer afternoon, and contemporary models do not demand a pair of trees for support. Rather, a sturdy metal stand, lightweight enough to be placed where it can be best enjoyed, is the current mode. The hammock itself can be readily unhitched for storage or replacement. Hammock styles also come in a variety of materials, ranging from woven types that let all the breezes through for a

Natural greenery along a privacy fence colors the background behind modern tubular-frame furniture on this combination wood and concrete patio.

Colorful cushions accent this patio bench, built of stock lumber and set against a privacy fence. Concrete poured in wood gridwork provides a surface suitable for all outdoor furniture types.

For out-and-out lounging, for sun, or for just plain relaxing, loungers come in a wide assortment of styles to suit most tastes. Some economy models may have one fixed position, but most are adjustable. Cushions in almost any style and color can be bought ready-made; many types are reversible for longer wear, or you can have them covered in a material of your own choosing. And when the time comes to re-cover them, these pads and cushions present no problem to the home seamstress. So long as the furniture itself is well constructed, periodic renewing of cushions and pads can keep these outdoor pieces looking fresh for years.

Loungers are for lounging. Unless you are pressed for seating space, it is not advisable to use loungers for seating purposes when serving food. Many a guest has been made to feel awkward and uncomfortable balancing a dinner plate on his lap while lying flat out on the latest model in patio furniture.

Some loungers are so luxurious that they can double as guest beds should you be faced by an unexpectedly large invasion of overnight visitors, or for any other emergency use. Children love them for slumber parties—they're smaller than beds so that you can cram several of them into a small space. And if you are fortunate enough to have a swimming pool, don't forget the inflatables as part of your outdoor-living furniture scheme.

Outdoor dining furniture. Dining outdoors can be as formal or as casual as you choose to make it, and there is an almost limitless variety of furniture to choose from. Tables may be round or rectangular; materials can range from wood to metal to plastic, or any combination of these that suits your

cooling effect to more luxurious, padded models that are softly upholstered for those who seek extra support while relaxing.

Swings and gliders—made primarily for use on porches where they can be suspended from ceiling rafters—are popular for those who want to seat several people in a small area. Another advantage: The movement of the swing or glider provides its own breeze on a warm night. But for true outdoor use, the glider is the obvious choice because it is free-standing with its own base. Gliders are available in natural finish, with weather-resistant varnish or lacquer, as well as in a wide range of colors (although you may want to repaint it to blend with, or match, a particular color scheme). Either way, gliders make sturdy, useful, and fun-type pieces of furniture for your outdoor living area.

A counter-high coping on this patio wall, set close to serving or cooking area, offers space for buffet trays that adds convenience to outdoor entertaining. A colorful patterned tablecloth enlivens the serving table.

life-style. For the family with young children, the classic picnic table and benches endure years of rugged wear. For large parties, put two of these picnic tables together to make a long banquet-type table—or as separate units, use one for the small fry and one for adults. For small areas, redwood tables are available in round styles, with or without a slot for an umbrella. Round tables enable you to seat more people in a smaller space than do rectangular models. Small chairs can be fitted around these round tables with ease; be sure to order a table that is supported pedestal-style so that there will be no legs or awkward corners to contend

When your lawn or patio party involves several tables, chairs of different designs can add interest and variety to the scene (right).

Metal outdoor furniture is both practical and decorative as used in this secluded patio.

with. All redwood furniture lends itself beautifully to relaxed, casual entertaining and everyday outdoor eating. And a big bonus that comes with it is easy maintenance—most redwood furniture has already been sealed and stained by the manufacturer, so that the wood is guaranteed to be weatherproof and the upkeep minimal.

Most metal furniture lends itself to a more formal style. Elegant wrought iron, formed into graceful chairs and tables with legs and supports that reflect leaf and flower designs, sets the mood for soft lights and flower-decked tables. Traditional white, black, and verdigris all lend themselves admirably to the outdoor scene and can be successfully combined with any color or color combination that suits your fancy. This is especially true when you are selecting patterns and designs for chair cushions, tablecloths, and

Old ice-cream-parlor type of chairs, painted white, and the popular sling chairs enhance this deck.

all the other accessories that make for a pleasing atmosphere. One tip to consider when buying metal outdoor furniture: Note carefully the *surface* of your patio before deciding on a definite style (see Chapter 7 for further information about this subject).

Lighting

There are many types of outdoor lights available today. All are attractive and easy to install (see Chapter 4 for information about electrical wiring). But they can do more than merely light your patio or deck. Not only will festive lights make a fairyland of your outdoor living space, but they can also attract what sometimes must seem like every mosquito and pesty bug alive in the universe! One easy solution to this everpresent problem is to use yellow bug-lights close to wherever you are sitting and put your bril-

Simple but functional outdoor furniture, enhanced by decorative plants and flowers, sets off this deck scene.

liant white lights some distance away. Then you and your guests can sit back and watch the insects gather around the white lights, leaving you in peace and comfort. Another method is to use old-fashioned kerosene lamps placed in the center of a table. Not only do they cast a soft, mellow glow across the table, illuminating it perfectly for dining, but kerosene lamps have a tendency to drive off insects. This is because of the slight aroma they give off—an aroma that will in no way be bothersome to you or your guests. Kerosene lamps also have wide bases that keep them from tipping over; and their glass chimneys, which can be found in colors as well as in clear glass, prevent the flame from blowing out in a breeze. Candles also make a lovely light, and windproof candle holders (hurricane-lamp style) made to blend with your outdoor motif are available in decorator and specialty shops. Or you can make your own candles, using oil-lamp chimneys, and thereby personalize your table setting. (A good tip for a candle that wobbles in its holder, whether homemade or not: With masking tape, wind the end of the candle that fits in the holder until you have a snug fit. This is better than melting candle wax into the holder, for that way you will eventually wind up with a candle cup clogged with old wax.)

Steps and paths need low-level light too, and lanterns can provide ample illumination for these spots as well. They may be placed among plantings, set at the edge of a step, or hung from low-hanging branches. Stands

Overhanging pierced metal lighting fixtures illuminate this attractive entranceway and patio.

from which to hang them at any desired height can be made by using ⅛-inch-diameter pipe, either black or galvanized, which is available from your plumbing supplier in 21-foot lengths (one length will make several stands). The pipe is easily cut with a hacksaw and can be bent in a vise to the form you want. Make the stand long enough so that it can be shoved deep into the ground for a secure footing. Mobility is an added advantage to these stands—they can be moved from place to place as occasion demands, and storage is no problem.

Patio torches will add another touch of glamor to outdoor entertaining on decks as well as patios. To use on a deck, simply stand the torch directly beside one of the railing posts, with the lower tip of the pole resting on the deck. Fasten the pole to the post in two places with conduit straps. If you prefer a longer pole, cut one from ½-inch thin-walled conduit, which is available in 10-foot lengths from an electrical supply house. These conduits fit most torches, but check yours before going ahead with the project. They can be especially useful when a wall or other obstruction makes inserting the torch at ground level impractical.

Most patio torches—and table lamps, too—are fueled with kerosene, which also acts to some degree as an insect repellent. Use them for general lighting on deck or patio or for any other area where electricity is impractical or undesirable.

If you prefer electricity for your outdoor lighting, a wide choice of fixtures is available. Post lanterns can be used instead of patio torches, and spotlights and floods (be sure you purchase outdoor types) can be employed for dramatic effects on the grounds—to illuminate a flower display, a fountain, or an entrance. For a gay and unusual decoration, use your outdoor Christmas lights—experiment with the various colored bulbs. The result can be charming. If you like overhead lights, there are available weatherproof pin sockets, sometimes called carnival lights, to mount on overhead wires plugged into an outdoor receptacle. (Check with your electrical supplier on connection details.) As detailed in Chapter 4, all outdoor lights and appliances *must* be plugged into weatherproof receptacles.

Table Settings

Let your imagination range when it's time to set the table for outdoor living. Remember that *you* should relax along with your family and guests, so don't tie yourself to items that require elaborate, time-consuming maintenance. Many of the newer plastic cloths and place mats are as pretty as those of the finest linen, and they are so easy to care for that there is really no excuse for a humdrum table setting. For a change of pace, try one of

The open-weave webbing on chairs and restrained color scheme of the table setting create a light, cool poolside arrangement.

the huge, oversized beach towels in a brilliant print for a tablecloth and, for napkins, use fingertip terry towels in a color (or colors) to mix and match. The absorbency of the terry cloth makes it a natural when serving some foods, and it couldn't be easier to care for—terry is natural wash and wear.

With your garden so close by, you can make having flowers on the table an everyday affair. To avoid crowding a small table, have some potted flowers nearby as part of the background; and in sheltered areas, tuck an occasional candle in among the blossoms for a smart effect. Push the candle base into the soil, and use tall candles so that their flames won't harm the blooms or set them on fire. (And don't forget to blow out the flames when you're finished!)

Other Equipment

For easy serving, a rolling cart, which can move food from house to deck or other outdoor dining area, is a great boon to the host or hostess. Especially useful is the type that has a lower shelf to hold soiled dishes and an electrical outlet to plug in a hot tray or coffee maker. Some carts with plug-in cords have their own hot top as well as an outlet.

Just as important as your food-warming equipment—along with barbecues and grills for actual cooking (see Chapter 7)—are coolers. A roomy, insulated container for ice cubes and another to hold cracked ice in which to pack bottled and canned refreshments make for added enjoyment. And if electricity is available, try a small portable

Sturdy but artistic, the chairs around this colorful flower-decorated table (right) have capped leg tips to prevent denting of the deck surface.

refrigerator, complete with a mobile stand, to roll out onto your deck, porch, or patio.

Another piece of outdoor electrical equipment that many people overlook is an electric fan. The most beautiful summer night can be hot and sultry, with not a trace of moving air. This can put a damper on the hardiest of summer enthusiasts. A strategically placed fan will produce a breeze that can make life worth living again. And there's another bonus—it will help keep the bugs away while you're coolong off!

Using Your Outdoor Living Area

Be sure to provide suitable protection from the elements for all your deck and patio furnishings and equipment. If there is a place to store them when they are not in use, do so by all means. Not all outdoor items need to be put away—cushions that can become waterlogged require it, along with other things that are not waterproof or that

Surrounding trees and shrubbery and fencing combine to create a cool secluded area for eating.

light and air to make the porch a pleasant place indeed on which to while away a summer afternoon or evening. Since everything is under shelter, there is less need for emergency covers or precautions against changes in the weather—and you won't ever have to face the problem of moving the party into the house in the midst of a sudden downpour.

House plants can play a natural role in traditional porch decor besides lending a decided outdoor living touch. The decor itself is a matter of your own choosing—it can be an extension of your house style, or it can be radically different, just as with your deck or patio. The important thing is that your porch should reflect *your* style of living; it should, above all, be a place where you feel comfortable, a place where you can enjoy the proximity of nature without suffering any of its disadvantages.

are so light in weight that they could blow away in a high wind. Waterproof covers, which are available for most standard outdoor furniture, can eliminate this chore. They are easy to put on and remove, so keep them handy, perhaps folded and tucked under the chair cushions. For winter storage of your outdoor furnishings, a permanent shelter is, of course, advisable.

Because porches are usually a combination of indoor and outdoor living areas, they lend themselves to a more conventional approach to entertaining. As a rule, all the equipment you need for easy service is at hand, along with an outdoor view that plays such an important part of the decor on decks and patios. Moreover, screens eliminate the insect problem, and wise use of various types of shades can control the amounts of

INDEX